SATISFYING THE EXPERIENCE OF HUNGER

RECOVERING THE SIGNIFICANCE OF THE RITE OF PRESENTATION OF THE GIFTS IN THE PHILIPPINE HUNGER SITUATION

CONTENTS

INTRODUCTION

One night, I had the experience of joining my brothers in De Paul House to distribute food to bridge dwellers in Munoz, Quezon City. These were people living perilously under the bridge whose lives were in danger when there was a typhoon. When we arrived at the place, many children and adults who waited for us for hours gathered around our car. We started to distribute one cup of rice and a viand to them. In just a few minutes, we ran out of supply. As I looked around, I saw a man lying on a piece of paper which served as his mat. I asked the person who was sitting beside him: *"Ano po ang nangyari sa kaniya?"* (What happened to him?) And he replied: *"masakit ang ulo at mataas po ang lagnat niya"* (He had a headache and fever). Then, I told his situation to my brother seminarian. We immediately looked for a pharmacy to buy medicine despite the heavy rains. We returned to the place and handed the medicine to him. After a few minutes of conversing with them, we left and returned to the seminary.

Pope Benedict XVI, during a summit of the United Nations Food and Agriculture Organization (FAO) in 2009 referred to hunger as "the most cruel and concrete sign of poverty." He must be worried about the hunger situation across the globe despite the abundance of resources. He called on the international community to discover new ways to combat the dreadful effects of hunger. The cry of the vulnerable and excluded: "I am hungry," is a plea not for indifference but for social justice, solidarity, and mutual responsibility. There are efforts by various international organizations, schools, NGOs, businesses, unions, and institutions to confront hunger. The Church too, by virtue of her pastoral mission, recognizes her participation to promote and improve the lives of the people. Yet, hunger continues to pose critical questions about the faith of the Church.

Interestingly, the Philippines is predominantly Christians. More than 86 percent of the total population belongs to the Roman Catholic religion. Paradoxically, the rich and the poor come together to celebrate the Eucharist. Thousands of people flock to the church every Sunday and hundred thousand Masses are celebrated in churches during *Simbang Gabi* and Holy Week, but hunger remains a serious problem that demands urgent attention and solution today. It is good to ask how it is possible that the country is largely Christians and celebrates the Eucharist every day without committing to the personal and societal liberation of people from hunger. Some of the questions that are being raised are: what causes hunger despite the abundance of wealth? How does the Church and State address hunger? How does the Eucharist become relevant to people who are experiencing hunger today? These questions have become enticing to theologians. The role of the theologians is to reflect the connections between the liturgy and life, between worship and praxis.

The Second Vatican Council declares that the Eucharist is the "source and summit of Christian life."[1] Put otherwise, the Eucharist is not merely an act of devotion, but it

[1] Lumen Gentium, 11

must be seen as central to the Christian life and worship. It is the pinnacle and summit of Christian lives to which everything is directed and from which everything flows. In its liturgical reforms, the Vatican II urges the faithful to "active, full and fruitful participation of the entire People of God in the eucharistic celebration.[2] "In the restoration and promotion of the sacred liturgy, this full and active participation by all the people is the aim to be considered before all else."[3] This 'active, full and conscious participation' by the faithful is not limited to liturgical celebrations but it has to be manifested even in social concerns. As argued by Monika Hellwig that "the simple, central action of the Eucharist is the sharing of food-not only eating but sharing. The simple, central human experience for the understanding of this action is hunger."[4] When the inherent values of the Eucharist are lived and applied, then it would be of great help to get rid of hunger.

Chapter One deals with the problem of hunger. It explores how the problem of hunger in the world becomes a phenomenon too that is inevitable in the Philippines. It highlights the various causes of shortage of food, the approaches of the secular organizations, the State, and the Church. Hence, the whole question of hunger could be viewed from the secular and magisterial sources.

Chapter Two studies the sources of the Rite of the Presentation of the Gifts by referring to Scripture, patristic writings of the Fathers of the Church, and Church's magisterial teachings. Here, the historical, analytical, descriptive, critical methods are employed in order to present a theological and praxis-oriented understanding of the Rite of the Presentation of the Gifts.

Chapter Three underscores the relevance of the Rite of the Presentation of the Gifts in the problem of hunger in the country. It establishes the connection between the Rite of the Presentation of the Gifts and hunger. Against this background, it stresses how the Rite plays a significant and transformative role in eradicating the problem of hunger in the Philippines.

---

[2] Austin Flannery, ed., *Dogmatic Constitution on the Sacred Liturgy Sacrosanctum Concilium,* Vatican Council II: The Conciliar and Post Conciliar Documents (Pasay City: Paulines, 2006), n. 155. Henceforth, this document shall be referred to as SC.

[3] SC, n. 14.

[4] Monika Hellwig, p. 2.

CHAPTER 1

Hunger in the Philippines

Hunger is a global and complex problem. Due to its harrowing and complex nature, hunger implies different understandings. For some who are physically hungry, food appeases them. When one hungers spiritually, only the divine can satisfy that hunger. While recognizing the different kinds of hunger, this paper, however, would like to limit itself to physical hunger, since this is basic in man and has an impact in the solidarity of the people as one nation. Hence, the interest of this research project is not spiritual but physical hunger.

This chapter explores the meaning of hunger according to Monika Hellwig. It also discusses the causes of hunger to have a comprehensive understanding of it. For a better view of the hunger situation, this chapter presents the global and local conditions. Next, the non-government organizations, the Philippine government, and Philippine Church undertake various responses to the problem of hunger. The chapter ends with a discussion on relevant documents on Catholic Social Teachings.

1. Hellwig's understanding of hunger

There are various definitions and perspectives which explain the concept in pursuit for the meaning of hunger. Hunger can be viewed as a desire for anything, craving for food, or lack of food. Such definitions focus on the *desire* to eat food. Others view hunger as an "uncomfortable or painful sensation caused by insufficient food energy consumption. Scientifically, hunger is referred to as food deprivation."[5] On the one hand, this view is more physiological because the body feels the unpleasant sensation when the person fails to eat enough food. The body needs enough dietary supplements to sustain its energy. On the other hand, it is understood in terms of *deprivation* of what the body needs so that it can function well according to its purpose. In short, hunger is both the deprivation and desire for food.

Going further, Monika Hellwig gives various insights on hunger which suit in the quest for meaning. She makes an explicit relationship between the Eucharist and the mission of the Church to the hungry. Her understanding of hunger is important as

[5] Food and Agriculture Organization (FAO), *Food Security Information for Action: Food Security Concepts and Framework* (European Union: FAO, 2008), 5. For additional information, see FAO, *Focus on Food Insecurity and Vulnerability: A Review of the UN System Common Country Assessment and World Bank Poverty Reduction Strategy Papers,* (FIVIMS Secretariat and Wageningen University and Research Centre) in www.fao.org/DOCREP/006/Y5095EOO.HTM. See also Stamoulis, Kostas and Alberto Zezza, *A Conceptual Framework for National Agricultural, Rural Development, and Food Security Strategies and Policies,* ESA Working Paper No. 03-17, November 2003, Agricultural and Development Economics Divisions, (Rome: FAO, 2003).

regards to the real meaning of the phenomenon under study. Hellwig agrees that "hunger is a total, global experience."[6] When a person feels hungry, it is not only the body that feels the distasteful sensation. The experience of hunger draws the attention of the whole person as he/she demands for food. The Filipino adage says, *"Ang sakit kalingkingan, sakit ng buong katawan"* (The pain of the little finger is felt by the whole body). Hunger, therefore, is not only felt by the body but the whole person.

Moreover, Hellwig describes hunger as "a painful experience. It is an experience of need, urgent need."[7] When an infant is hungry, he/she is crying and screaming. A child becomes ill-tempered when the food is served late. It is a painful experience that calls for an urgent response to satisfy the basic need for food. However, hunger can be "functional."[8] There are those who opt to fast for a period because of advocacies and religious practice. Mahatma Gandhi fasted many times as a non-violent reaction to the government. The Catholic Church too obliges its members to practice fasting and abstinence during Lenten Season.

Finally, Hellwig states that "hunger is the most basic experience of dependence, of contingency, of the need for others."[9] When a person experiences hunger, he/she too is experiencing inadequacy and having needs. Human dependence characterizes hunger. Hunger "brings into focus human dependence on the bounty of nature... and brings into focus the human person's dependence on other human beings."[10] Human beings need vegetables, fruits, meat, fish, among others, for survival. Yet, it is also a dependence on others. A hungry person knows that he/she cannot be fed without the cooperation of others. If only people are responsive to the needs of hungry people, it is most probable that hunger can be alleviated. In short, hunger is both deprivation and desire. Hellwig adds another dimension of hunger, that is, dependence.

But people become unaware about hunger and the need to be satisfied when food and drink become available. Hellwig notes: "Our hunger is satisfied so quickly, so easily, so continuously that we can easily forget that hunger is there at all; it does not intrude itself."[11] Consequently, people become indifferent and do not show concern and affection to the hungry because of the satisfaction they experience from the abundance of food. Care for the hungry escapes the compassion of those who have experienced abundance of life. Patrick McCormick argues therefore that people feel sympathy and compassion to the hungry people when they recognize that they are hungry eaters and acknowledge their neediness.[12] Thus, Hellwig concludes: "to be human is to be hungry. Not to be hungry is to be dead."[13]

---

[6] Monika K. Hellwig, *The Eucharist and the Hunger of the World* (New York: Paulist Press, 1976), 4. Hellwig understands the Eucharist not only as eating but more importantly as sharing.

[7] Hellwig, *The Eucharist and the Hunger of the World*, 5.

[8] Ibid., 5.

[9] Hellwig, *The Eucharist and the Hunger of the World*, 6.

[10] Ibid., 4.

[11] Ibid., 3.

[12] Patrick T. McCormick, *A Banqueter's Guide to the All-Night Soup Kitchen of the Kingdom of God* (Collegeville, MN: Liturgical Press, 2004), 7.

[13] Hellwig, *The Eucharist and the Hunger of the World*, 3.

2. Hunger in the World, Asia, and the Philippines

Having a clear understanding of what hunger is, it is good to see in a greater picture the whole problem of hunger in the society. Hunger, as seen below, cuts across in various parts of the world. It is a problem that calls for focused efforts and concerted attention. In the next subsequent sections, one can investigate how serious the problem of hunger is, based on the data which are being presented below. However, hunger is considered a problem too in the Philippines.

2.1. World Hunger

Hunger is a daily reality in the world. According to the United Nations Food and Agriculture Organization (FAO), about 842 million people or 12% of the global population were unable to meet their dietary energy requirements in 2011-2013. [14] One out of eight of the world's population is suffering from hunger and not enough food for a healthy life. The latest update by FAO says that "world hunger is on the rise [since] the estimated number of undernourished people increased from 777 million in 2015 to 815 million in 2016."[15] This figure is alarming and distressing as more and more people do not have access to food. They are susceptible to disease and death due to deficiencies of nutrients. Most of the hungry people live in lower-middle-income countries like South Sudan, Somalia, Yemen, and northeast Nigeria where there is a high risk of famine.[16]

The most affected by hunger are the children. The child undernutrition continues to decline yet "overweight among children under five is becoming more of a problem in most regions, and adult obesity continues to rise in all regions."[17] Among children, there are 154.8 million under the age of five who are suffering from stunted growth; 51.7 million children are affected by wasting; 40.6 million children who are overweight; and adult obesity has reached to 640.9 million people. [18] This data shows the conditions of hunger in the world. It is a social problem that calls for deeper reflections and concerted efforts.

---

[14] F ood and Agriculture Organization (FAO), International Fund for Agricultural Development (IFAD) and World Food Programme (WFP), *The State of Food Insecurity in the World 2013: The Multiple Dimensions of Food Insecurity* (Rome: FAO, 2013), 15.

[15] Food and Agriculture Organization (FAO), International Fund for Agricultural Development (IFAD) and World Food Programme (WFP), United Nations Children's Fund (UNICEF), World Health Organization (WHO), *The State of Food Security and Nutrition in the World 2017* (Rome: FAO, 2017).

[16] David Beckmann and Arthur Simon, *Grace at the Table: Ending Hunger in God's World* (New York: Paulist Press,1999), 16.

[17] FAO, IFAD and WFP, *The State of Food Security and Nutrition in the World 2017.*

[18] FAO, IFAD and WFP, *The State of Food Security and Nutrition in the World 2017.*

2.2. Asia

Although Africa is known for hunger, Asia has the highest population in the world with the greatest number of people who are exposed to poverty, hunger, and malnourishment. Asia is more populated as compared to other continents in the world. It has the greatest number of malnourished children. It increased from 9.4 percent in 2015 to 11.5 percent in 2016 which comprises 70 percent of all malnourished children in the world. Thus, the children in Asia are most likely underweight compared to children anywhere else in the world.

According to FAO, in 2016 almost 512 million people were still hungry in Asia.[19] A big chunk of the total of the world's hungry people belongs to Southern Asia with 218.4 million undernourished people.[20] In Eastern Asian and South-eastern Asia, undernourished people are 11.3 million and 27.8 million respectively. But the countries which are greatly affected by food crises are Afghanistan, Iraq, Syria, and Yemen due to conflicts that have displaced the lives of the people as well as disrupted their livelihoods. The data from the official statistics on hunger incidence indicate that hunger has been worsening in Asia. The Philippines too has a high incidence of hunger.

2.3. Philippines

As part of Asia, the Philippines is concerned about the widespread and increasing hunger incidence in recent years. Despite the high growth rates trumpeted by the administration, it is still confronted with issues of hunger and poverty. Evidence from official statistics and national surveys of hunger by the Social Weather Stations (SWS) suggest that the Philippines has been struggling to address the perennial problem of hunger. For instance, the SWS survey conducted during the 1st Quarter of 2018 concludes that "9.9 percent or an estimated 2.3 million families suffered hunger from January to March, down from 3.6 million in the last quarter of 2017."[21] Although there has been progress in reducing hunger in the country, the fact remains that hunger is still a big problem in the country. It is also ironic that the country is rich with natural resources, but the number of hungry people is still very high. Few wealthy families like Henry Sy, Lucio Tan, and Ayala, among others, own a big share in the wealth of the nations.

Nonetheless, it is unfortunate that the children are the victims of this hunger situation. The 7th National Nutrition Survey (NNS) of 2008 conducted by the Food Nutrition and Research Institute revealed that in the year 2008 the number of underweight children aged 0-5 has increased to 26.2 million. The latest survey discloses

---

[19] FAO, IFAD and WFP, *The State of Food Security and Nutrition in the World 2017*.

[20] FAO, IFAD and WFP, *The State of Food Security and Nutrition in the World 2017*.

[21] Julius N. Leonen, "Hunger Falls in First Quarter of 2018-SWS," *Philippine Daily Inquirer,* https://www.google.com.ph/amp/s/newsinfo.inquirer.net/986324/breaking-news-sws-hunger-rodrigo-duterte-gloria-macapagal-arroyo/amp (accessed 6.12.2018).

that 3.7 million of the 11.2 million children aged 0-5 years in 2015 suffered from malnutrition which "has adverse effects on crucial stages of child development, leading to cognitive and behavioral deficits, learning disability, and ultimately to an uncompetitive workforce."[22] Poor children who are not provided with enough food are less attentive to parents and teachers because their learning ability is affected. Some of them too may possibly commit violent crimes when their brain and stomach are not fed well. In other words, if malnutrition persists, the children may not have a good and healthy life in the future. Ultimately, society may pay a price for the failure to feed the poor children- a price that costs more than the problem of hunger and malnutrition.

From the above discussion, one can see the instances which may lead to hunger. These are the natural calamities which continuously affected the country; the culture of corruption in the country; increase of foreign debt due to international loans; the unequal distribution of the country's wealth as the rich become richer while the poor become poorer, and the poverty experienced by the people.

3. Causes of Hunger

There are various factors that contribute to hunger in the country. These causes mentioned below are only some of the many factors that have caused hunger. These reasons of hunger studied below are natural calamities, poverty, armed conflict, corruption, and lack of social justice. They are discussed against the background of the Eucharist as a model of transformation.

3.1. Natural calamities

One important cause of hunger in the Philippines is the prevalence of natural calamities like typhoons, floods, and droughts. Sadly, the Philippines is the most exposed country to these natural disasters because of its location in the Pacific.[23] In Metro Manila, which is below sea level, continuous heavy rain results in flooding in every part of Manila. These natural disasters have devastating effects on the agricultural lands and crops of the country because they result in a decline in agricultural productivity which eventually becomes a threat to the livelihood of the poor.

Additionally, to the farmers whose main source of living is farming, typhoons and drought influence the quantity and quality of their farm production. Briones and Israel, argue that natural disasters have negative impacts on agriculture. For them, natural disasters can "reduce farm productivity, damage farm inputs and facilities, limit farm

---

[22] Roehlano Briones et al, *Food Security and Nutrition in the Philippines* (Manila: Brain Trust, INC., 2017), 1, 11-29. This strategic review on food security in the Philippines was an independent review commissioned by the World Food Programme (WFP).

[23] Sophie Brown, "The Philippines Is the Most Storm-Exposed Country on Earth," http://world.time.com/2013/11/11/the-philippines-is-the-most-storm-exposed-country-on-earth,(accessed 8.3.2018).

planting options, damage farm supply routes, and markets, and cause death and injury to farm workers."[24] These natural disasters have a significant effect on the poor's standard of living which results in hunger.

3.2. Poverty

Another significant devastating cause of hunger is poverty. Poverty can be understood as the state of not having enough resources and access to the basic needs in life like shelter, education, and food. Sen argues that poverty is seen as "a deprivation of basic capabilities, rather than merely as low income."[25] The poor become poor because they lack the capacity to purchase and to access the necessities. He further views poverty in its relatedness to inequality. He said that "[t]o view poverty as an issue in inequality, as is often recommended, seems to do little justice to either concept. Poverty and inequality relate closely to each other, but they are distinct concepts and can neither subsume the other."[26] If inequality and the lack of purchasing power persist, then this may create situations of hunger. Hunger, therefore, is one of the effects of poverty. Thus, poverty and hunger are closely related.

In the Philippines, the poverty rate is high due to various factors like corruption, unequal income distribution, and lack of resources. The Philippine government is exhausting all efforts to improve the economy, but every effort seems to result in failure. Funds intended to uplift the life of the poor people end up in the pockets of politicians. The government money for the poverty programs is not properly utilized. As a result, the gap between the rich and poor is continuously widening which results in several people feeling hungry in various places in the country. In the latest survey conducted by Social Weather Stations in the 4th quarter of 2017, it shows that 44% or an estimated 10 million families considered themselves as poor.[27] Many people in the country are still living below the poverty line despite the growth in the economy and abundance of natural resources. They cannot afford to buy nutritious food for themselves and their families.

3.3. Armed Conflict

In his annual address to the United Nations' Food and Agriculture Organization on World Food Day last October 16, 2017, Pope Francis is convinced that hunger can only be fought by going to the root cause of the problem. He identifies conflicts as one of the root causes of the problem of hunger. He said: "It's clear that wars and climate

---

[24] Israel C. Danilo, Roehlano M. Briones, "Impacts of Natural Disasters on Agriculture, Food Security, and Natural Resources," *Economic Research Institute for ASEAN and East Asia Discussion Paper Series 15* (2013): 4.

[25] Amartya Sen, *Development as Freedom* (New York: Anchor Books, 1999), 20.

[26] Amartya Sen, *Poverty and Famines: An Essay on Entitlement and Deprivation* (London, New York, Toronto: Oxford University Press, 1984), 22-23.

[27] Janvic Mateo, "SWS: 1 in 3 Families Move Out of Poverty," *The Philippine Star,* January 21, 2018, https://www.philstar.com/headlines/2018/01/21/1779850/sws-1-3-families-move-out-poverty, (accessed 12.7.2018).

change cause hunger; let us stop presenting it as an incurable illness."[28] Conflicts are creating famine and food insecurity.

The Philippines is struggling with the longstanding armed conflicts, that is, against the communist insurgency and against the *Bangsa Moro rebellion* (Moro National Liberation Front and Moro Islamic Liberation Front) which takes massive spending on the armed forces that could have been utilized for food and other basic needs. Ultimately, the armed conflict has resulted in the displacement of families, and the devastation of livelihood. Surely, extreme hunger is a problem in places where there is displacement and destruction of livelihood, especially in Mindanao. Many people are migrating to other places and have lost their homes because of war and violence. Also, it affects agricultural production, reduces food availability, and disrupts the flow of the market. These hostilities and conflict lead to poverty and hunger.

Nonetheless, Byron argues that "…if less were spent to purchase or produce arms, more would be available to purchase or produce bread for the world."[29] To counterattack insurgencies, the government is spending too much money on military equipment in combating the armed conflicts in the country. Although there are initiatives by the government for peace talks, the results of these negotiations are yet to be reaped. Thus, the people are not benefiting from the country's resources because a big chunk of the budget is allocated to military expenditures. The poor are primarily the victims of this local war. As a result, more and more people are suffering from hunger.

3.4. Social Injustice

One of the main causes of hunger is social justice since the poor people are deprived of gaining access to the means which help them uplift their economic and social status. From the time of Spaniards until now, the poor people are not given the means to improve their lot. For instance, most of the land of the nation is owned by a few wealthy families while the majority Filipinos only owned a portion of this land. Or the land reform program of the government which intends to provide land for people for their survival is hardly implemented because the landlords do not want to lose their income from the lands. Only the rich people control the resources of the land. The land is important for people to survive. Here, the concern of social justice is at the pedestal. The unequal sharing of wealth among people is due to grave social injustice. Social justice demands that ownership of the goods of the country be equally accessible to all. Nicole Ball believes that "the roots of global hunger are to be found in socio-economic and political inequality."[30]

---

[28] Francis, *Address to the United Nations' Food and Agriculture Organization on Word Food Day,* (16 October 2017), http://m.vatican.va/content/francescomobile/en/speeches/2017/october/documents/papa-francesco_20171016_visita-fao.html (accessed 5.13.2018).

[29] William J. Byron, "The Causes of World Hunger," in *The Causes of World Hunger,* ed. William J. Byron (Ramsey, NJ: Paulist, 1982): 5-15, 10.

[30] Nicole Ball, *World Hunger: A Guide to the Economic and Political Dimensions* (Santa Barbara, Cali: American Bibliographical Center, Clio Press, 1981), 202.

3.5. Corruption

Corruption is endemic in the Philippines. Sadly, the Philippines is branded as one of the corrupt countries yet ironically the majority are Christians. There are many reasons for corruption. For instance, the corrupt practice called "standard operating procedure" (SOP) for the people in politics is rampant. Unfortunately, one consequence of corruption is that it worsens income inequality and poverty.[31] This massive corruption in the country perpetrated by the corrupt people both in the public and private sector is causing poverty. When there is no poverty, the people will have the resources to feed their families. The 2013 survey made by the Office of the Ombudsman showed that there is poverty because of corruption.[32] It ranks 95th among 168 countries in Transparency International's Corruption Perceptions Index 2015.[33] The World Bank in its 2001 report is convinced that the end of corruption leads to poverty reduction, better delivery of social services, and quality infrastructure.[34] The resources that could have been used for quality education, good infrastructure, and better health care and other social services are diverted to the corrupt bureaucrats and employees. The poor sectors of the society who need these basic services become the direct victims of corruption. Corruption is often a contributing factor to hunger in the country.

Obviously, there are other factors that contribute to widespread hunger. It is good to note that hunger can be reduced in the country when the multiple causes of hunger mentioned above are solved and addressed. These causes of hunger have merely human influences which can be ameliorated. Besides, hunger has been so far neglected which leads to its continuous worsening. The next section deals with the focused efforts made by various institutions to address hunger in the country.

4. Various responses to Hunger

The world is not blinded by the problem of hunger. Hunger is a serious problem that calls for insistent attention from various institutions. It is a concern of all, not just to those who are greatly affected by it. The various approaches to hunger are categorized into non-government institutions and the international community, the Philippine government, the Philippine Church, and the Catholic Social Thought. Both the Church and State compliment and collaborate with each other to eradicate hunger in the country.

---

[31] Paolo Mauro, "Causes and Consequences of Corruption" in *Ehem!: A Manuel For Deepening Involvement in Combating Corruption,* 2nd ed. (Quezon City: Philippine Province of the Society of Jesus, Committee on the Evangelization of Culture, 2003) 30.

[32] Aika Rey, "In Numbers: Impact of Corruption on the Philippines," *Rappler*, 10 August 2016, https://www.google.com.ph/amp/samp.rappler.com/move-ph/issues/corruption/141391-impact-corruption-philippines (accessed 7.6.2017).

[33] Ibid.

[34] Ibid.

4.1. Non-government Institutions and International Community's Response to Hunger

Nonetheless, the increase of world hunger poses a significant challenge for the international and local community. This drive against hunger is a shared responsibility and commitment by all. To respond to this challenge, the United Nations has initiated various programs that made a significant impact to eradicate hunger.

The Food and Agriculture Organization (FAO) is the lead agency in the United Nations whose task is to "alleviate poverty and hunger by promoting agricultural development, improved nutrition and the pursuit of food security...for an active and healthy life."[35] In collaboration with FAO, the United Nations International Children Education Fund (UNICEF) was created in 1946 to "provide emergency food and health care to children in countries that had been ravaged by World War II."[36] Later on, it has "evolved from an emergency fund to a development agency, committed to protecting the rights of every child to survival, protection, and development."[37]

Furthermore, in 1974 United Nations World Food Conference in Rome, the governments adopted the Universal Declaration on the Eradication of Hunger and Malnutrition, thus proclaim, "every man, woman and child have the inalienable right to be free from hunger and malnutrition in order to develop their physical and mental faculties."[38] The goal of this conference is to eradicate hunger in all nations. Hence, the conference called for concerted global efforts among the members of the international community to eradicate hunger and to achieve sustainable food security that is available for all. In response to the World Food Conference, the International Fund for Agriculture Development (IFAD) was established in 1977. The IFAD has the responsibility to alleviate hunger and poverty in developing countries by providing loans and grants to poor countries for the agricultural projects for the poor.[39]

In 1996, nations were convened for the World Food Summit amidst the pervasive hunger. In that conference, the governments made their commitment: "We pledge our political will and our common and national commitment to achieving food security for all and to an ongoing effort to eradicate hunger in all countries, with an immediate view to

---

[35] United Nations, *Basic Facts About the United Nations* (New York: United Nations Publication, 2004), 42.

[36] Ibid., 36.

[37] Ibid., 36.

[38] United Nations, "Universal Declaration on the Eradication of Hunger and Malnutrition," https://www.ohchr.org/en/professionalinterest/pages/eradicationofhungerandmalnutrition.aspx (accessed 7.21.2018). This Universal Declaration on the Eradication of Hunger and Malnutrition was adopted last November 16, 1974 by the nations who attended the World Food Conference that was convened under General Assembly Resolution 3180 (XXVIII) of December 17, 1973 and eventually endorsed by General Assembly Resolution 3348 (XXIX) of December 17, 1974.

[39] United Nations, *Basic Facts About the United Nations*, 50.

reducing the number of undernourished people to half their present level no later than 2015."[40]

Likewise, in September 2015, the 193 UN Member States committed to Sustainable Development Goals including to "end hunger, achieve food security and improved nutrition and promote sustainable agriculture" by 2030.[41] These efforts made by various agencies have counteracted the harrowing problem of hunger in the world. The Philippines is also a member of the United Nations and is sharing this goal of alleviating hunger.

4.2. Response of the Philippine Government to Hunger

The government's role is important because there are things which the private institutions cannot do due to their limitations. For this reason, the government has a prime responsibility to address the state of hunger and malnutrition in the country. Among the concrete steps of the government are the implementation of *RA 6657: Comprehensive Agrarian Reform Law (1988)* which allows the "distribution of land to landless farmers;" *RA 7607: Magna Carta for Small Farmers (1992)* which aims to "promote the socio-economic development of small farmers;" *RA 8976: Philippine Food Fortification Act of 2000* which "fortifies with essential micronutrients staple food items like rice, flour, oil and sugar."[42]

Under the administration of the current president, Rodrigo Duterte, Executive Order No. 5 was signed last October 2016 which provides the adoption of *"Ambisyon Natin* 2040," a long-term vision for the country in the next 25 years. Under this vision, the Philippines aspires that the Filipinos will live and "enjoy a strongly rooted, comfortable and secure life" where "no one is poor, no one is ever hungry."[43] This is an effort made by the Philippine government to assure that food is available for all in the years to come which eventually improves the quality of lives of the people.

To carry out this goal, the government has formed the Philippine Plan of Action for Nutrition (2017-2022) in which the Local Government Units, in collaboration with different government institutions, are provided funds for feeding programs.[44] To institutionalize this feeding program for undernourished children in public daycare centers, *"Masustansyang Pagkain Para Sa Batang Pilipino* Act" or Republic Act No. 11037

[40] Food and Agriculture Organization, "Rome Declaration on World Food Security and World Food Summit Plan of Action," http://www.fao.org/docrep/003/w3613e/w3613e00.htm#PoA (accessed 21.3.2018). See also the World Food Summit after five years in http://www.fao.org/monitoringprogress/index_en.html.

[41] Food and Agriculture Organization, "Sustainable Development Goals," http://www.fao.org/sustainable-development-goals/en/ (accessed 3.8.2018).

[42] Cesar Garcia, "Fast Facts: What Has the Government Done to Alleviate Malnutrition?," *Rappler*, https://www.rappler.com/newsbreak/iq/208157-what-philippine-government-has-done-address-malnutrition (accessed 28.10.2018).

[43] National Economic and Development Authority, "Ambisyon Natin 2014, A Long Term Vision for the Filipinos," in http://2040.neda.gov.ph/about-ambisyon-natin-2040/ (accessed 3.8.2018).

[44] National Nutrition Council, "Philippine Plan of Action for Nutrition 2017-2022," in http://www.nnc.gov.ph/phocadownloadpap/PPAN/18Sept_PPAN2017_2022Executive%20Summary.pdf (accessed 19.5.2018).

signed into law last June 29, 2018. Similarly, the "Build Build Build" program of the Duterte Administration which improves the infrastructures of the country and promises to create more jobs for the Filipino people is an effort by the government to help reduce the nation's hunger.

Likewise, the government is continuously implementing a Conditional cash transfer program- the *Pantawid Pamilyang Pilipino Program (4Ps)* for the poorest of the poor in the Philippines. It aims to provide conditional cash grants to 20 million Filipinos so they can combat poverty and hunger.[45] All of these programmes of the government, thus, aim to eradicate poverty and hunger in the country. If this is done, there is hope that the Filipino people live a comfortable life.

4.3. Response of the Philippine Church to hunger

The Philippine Church too is very much aware of the problem of hunger in the country. True to its prophetic mission of announcing and teaching the message of God, the Church responds to the challenges of the time through reflection and action. Social justice, equal distribution of goods and options for the poor are central to the Philippine Church through the years. The Church, therefore, is confronting the challenges of the time through a deeper and wider social consciousness among the faithful. Pastoral Letters and Statements of the Catholic Bishops Conference of the Philippines (CBCP) are of great importance to raise the people's social consciousness.

4.4. Pastoral Letter of the Philippine Catholic Hierarchy on "Social Justice" (1949)

The Pastoral Letter of the bishops rightly states that "the world belongs to all men, not just to a few."[46] It further recognizes that "to all men during their time of pilgrimage and trial on earth God has given the means of living in accord with the lofty dignity and duties of their state as rational beings and children of God."[47] In other words, the earth and wealth which are for all must serve the needs of men and women in accordance with their dignity. They have the right to decent living and sufficiency of decent food that God has given to men and women.[48] This right assures that the material goods that the people need must be fulfilled in a manner suitable to human dignity. It is not selfishness and greed that rules the goods of the earth. It is justice and common

---

[45]World Bank, "FAQs About the Pantawid Pamilyang Pilipino Programs (4Ps)," https://www.worldbank.org/en/country/philippines/brief/faqs-about-the-pantawid-pamilyang-pilipino-program (accessed accessed 10.9. 2018).

[46] Catholic Bishops of the Philippines, *A Joint Pastoral Letter of the Catholic Bishops of the Philippines on Social Justice,* (May 21, 1949). For other documents of the Catholic Bishops Conference of the Philippines from 1940's up to the present, see https://cbcpwebsite.com/index.html.

[47] Ibid.

[48] Ibid.

good that permeates these goods. In the absence of these two important principles, hunger persists.

4.5. Pastoral Statement of the Philippine Hierarchy on "Year of Social Action," (1968)

The Catholic Bishops Conference of the Philippines (CBCP) asserts that "material resources entail a stewardship" yet this stewardship is betrayed "by vulgar display and consumption of resources that lead to the scandal of the unemployed and the hungry."[49] In other words, greed for the nation's wealth is one of the greatest contributing factors to hunger. Social justice demands that the wealth of the nation does not belong to only a few but to all the people. To ensure equity of wealth, the Philippine Church urges the government to implement the land reform program so that the people may enjoy their basic right to food.[50]

4.6. Pastoral Exhortation on the Philippine Economy (1997)

Moreover, in the 1997 Asian economic crisis, the CBCP issued a Pastoral Exhortation on the Philippine Economy in which it asserts that economic development must have a human face. The poor who are in situations of poverty and hunger must be the central aim of development. These people who are experiencing hunger and poverty have a God-given dignity that ought to be acknowledged. What the Philippine Church aspires to is a "caring economy." It is an economy that does not bring marginalization and exploitation but total human development and poverty alleviation.

4.7. Social Action

The CBCP's Commission on Social Apostolate is working for the development of greater awareness of social consciousness among the people. To be more effective, the programs of the Social Apostolate must be infused in the diocesan programs. The diocesan social action centers must be avenues to implement programs for social concerns. Also, various charitable institutions are established to respond to social problems. For example, Caritas Manila, a Catholic charity of the Archdiocese of Manila, has fed 36,997 undernourished children through its feeding program. It continues to provide support to children who are undernourished through its various programs. Additionally, the Catholic Relief Services (CRS) which has been operating in the Philippines since 1945 has been active in food supplement programs for the malnourished children in the country. The CRS's policy states that "the policies and

---

[49] Catholic Bishops' Conference of the Philippines, *Pastoral Statement of the Philippine Hierarchy on Year of Social Action,* (May 1, 1968).

[50] Ibid.

programs of the agency reflect and express the teaching of the Catholic Church. At the same time, CRS assists based on need, not creed, race or nationality."[51] Different religious communities are also helping to end hunger. For example, the De Paul House community in Tandang Sora, Quezon City is institutionalizing the "Soup Kitchen" as a share in the fight against hunger. Inspired by St. Vincent de Paul, the seminarians are distributing food to the street dwellers every night. All these efforts are undertaken as a response to this social concern.

4.8. Response of Catholic Social Teaching of the Church to Hunger

For many years, the Church has been engaged in the social, cultural, political, and economic life of the people. Through its analyses, reflections, judgements, and actions which are based on the Gospel and Traditions, the Church responds to the emerging complex challenges of times. The Church is neither *against* nor *of* the world, but it is *in* the world that is actively involved and immersed in the human experiences of the poor.[52] Against this background, the Catholic Social Teaching forms into one proclaimed official teachings of the Church about the reflections and discernment of the various issues that confront human beings. Hence, it is good to understand the relevance and impact of Catholic Social Teaching on the problem of hunger.

4.9. Rerum Novarum

Through the ages, the Church has been greatly involved in battling with the social issues that continue to disturb and distress the people. Hunger is one of them. Hence, the Church, through the popes' magisterial pronouncements, started to speak to the world on social issues that afflict the people's lives. *Rerum Novarum* of Leo XIII in 1891 is the written articulation of various ideas and reflections on social concerns which "set in motion the tradition of the popes continuing to address the social problems of the day."[53]

One of the many elements of *Rerum Novarum* is the relationship between the Church and the poor. The Church is not purely concerned about the eternal salvation of the poor; it is also concerned about their temporal needs.[54] These temporal needs of the poor include the satisfaction of their necessities like food. The Church desires "that the poor, for example, should rise above poverty and wretchedness, and should better their

---

[51] Catholic Relief Services (CRS), https://www.interaction.org/member/catholic-relief-services (accessed 10.8.2010). The Catholic Relief Services which was established in 1943 by the Catholic Bishops of the United States, aims to give assistance to the people who are in need outside the United States.

[52] Pilario, CM, (ed.), *Faith in Action: Catholic Social Teaching on the Ground*, 26.

[53] Thomas Shannon, "Commentary on Rerum Novarum (The Condition of Labor)," in *Modern Catholic Social Teaching: Commentaries and Interpretations,* ed. Kenneth R. Himes, OFM (Washington: Georgetown University Press, 2011), 127.

[54] Ibid., 137.

condition in life; and for this, it strives."[55] In short, the Church must exhibit sensibilities towards the poor in order to fortify their welfare for "charity, as a virtue, belongs to the Church."[56] In the interest of the poor, the Church is vigorously undertaking works of charity to eliminate hunger and poverty.

In the same way, to end poverty and hunger is not only the responsibility of the Church; the State too has a legitimate role in addressing these social concerns. The State must ensure "that the laws and institutions, the general character and administration of the commonwealth, shall be such as to produce for themselves public well-being and private prosperity."[57] These laws and institutions must serve human needs. But the most challenging obligation of the State towards the poor is "to act with strict justice..."[58] To act on justice, the interests and well-being of the poor must be protected by the State. In short, to eradicate hunger the Church and State must work together in unity.

4.10. *Gaudium et Spes*

One of the most powerful constitutions of Vatican II is the *Gaudium et Spes:* Pastoral Constitution on the Church in the Modern World which was promulgated on December 7, 1965. It is significant in the Church because it "is an attempt to read the signs of the times so that the church can articulate its best hopes for humanity."[59] By reading the situation of humanity, the Church is opening itself to the contemporary world so that the Church can learn from the world and the world can learn from the Church. Hence, this document allows the Church to be in constant interaction and dialogue with the experiences in the light of the gospel.

Just at its beginning, *Gaudium et Spes* already expresses its whole message: "The joys and the hopes, the grief and anguish of the people in our time, especially those who are poor and afflicted, are the joys and hopes, the grief and anguish of the followers of Christ."[60] Not only thus the Church is concerned about the joys and hopes of the world, the Church too is concerned about the critical social issues like hunger and poverty which are the 'anguish and grief of the people.' To respond to the challenges of hunger and poverty is a necessary obligation of the Church for its mission is to uplift people's lives.

---

[55] Leo XIII, Encyclical on the Condition of the Working Classes *Rerum Novarum* (15 May 1891), no. 23 (Boston, MA: Daughter of St Paul, 2000).

[56] *Rerum Novarum,* no. 24.

[57] *Rerum Novarum,* no. 26.

[58] *Rerum Novarum,* no. 27.

[59] David J. O'Brien and Thomas A. Shannon, *Catholic Social Thought; Documentary Heritage* (New York: Orbis Books, 2010), 172.

[60] Vatican Council II, Pastoral Constitution on the Church in the Modern World *Gaudium et Spes* (7 December 1965), no. 1, in Vatican Council II: The Conciliar and Post Conciliar Documents, Austin Flannery, ed., (Pasay City: Paulines, 2006). The Second Vatican Council, the twenty first Ecumenical Council of the Church, was announced and convened by John XXIII on 11 October, 1962 to embark on genuine *aggiornamento.* One of the conciliar documents which was promulgated in 1965 by Paul VI was the *Gaudium et Spes.* It focused on the need to dialogue the Church with the world.

Nevertheless, the Second Part of the document discusses socio-economic life which reiterates that the world is confronted with economic and social inequalities between individuals and nations. Guided by the principles of justice and equity, *Gaudium et Spes* urges the Christian members of the Church to be true to its mission of working together to abate the gap between the rich and the poor. In the words of *Gaudium et Spes*: "God intended the earth and all that it contains for the use of every human being and people. Thus, as all men follow justice and unite in charity, good should abound for them on a reasonable basis."[61] These earth's resources are created by God to meet human needs. In the *Gaudium et Spes* reminds the people in the words of the Church Fathers: "

> Feed the man dying of hunger, because if you have not fed him you have killed him and it urges them according to their ability to share and dispose of their goods to help others, above all by giving them aid which will enable them to help and develop themselves."[62]

To help the hungry is not a choice but a responsibility that needs to be undertaken. The goods of the earth must be used and shared with others to uplift their misery.

4.11. Populorum Progressio

Two years after the closure of Vatican II in 1965, Paul VI wrote a very important document called *Populorum Progressio* that places the social question into a wider perspective. Paul VI stresses the relationship of development which is understood in its social and economic sense; this development is the path to peace. Precisely, this development is social because every individual is an essential part of the larger society. True development, the Pope asserts, includes the acquisition of the necessities of life. Food is one of the necessities of life and so no wonder that Paul VI pays attention to the problem of hunger in the world. His words were:

> Today no one can be ignorant any longer of the fact that in whole continents countless men and women are ravaged by hunger, countless numbers of children are undernourished, so that many of them die in infancy, while the physical growth and mental development of many others are retarded and as a result whole regions are condemned to the most depressing despondency.[63]

[61] Vatican Council II, *Gaudium et Spes*, no. 69.

[62] Vatican Council II, *Gaudium et Spes*, no. 69.

[63] Paul VI, Encyclical On the Development of Peoples *Populorum Progressio*: (26 March 1967), no. 45 (Boston, MA: Daughter of St. Paul, 2000). In the first paragraph of *Populorum Progressio*, the word "hunger" has appeared which shows that the Church, as her important mission, is very much concerned on this social problem.

From the words of Paul VI, hunger is perceived to be one of the confronting issues that the world needs to address so that true development is achieved. Although the Church is closely responding to this problem, each one has an equal share in the efforts to alleviate hunger. Paul VI says: "today the peoples in hunger are making a dramatic appeal to the peoples blessed with abundance. The Church shudders at this cry of anguish and calls each one to give a loving response of charity towards this brother's cry for help."[64] In reference to the principle of solidarity, the Pope urges both the local and international communities to deal with the challenges of poverty and hunger; and impels the Church to make contributions to human development. But the goal of this Christian duty is not to eliminate hunger but to build a world where everyone "can live a fully human life" freed from servitude to the rich and powerful.[65]

4.12. *Sollicitudo Rei Socialis*

To commemorate the twentieth anniversary of *Populorum Progressio,* John Paul II wrote an encyclical *Sollicitudo Rei Socialis* (On Social Concern) on December 30, 1987. After twenty years of *Populorum Progressio's* publication, John Paul II observes that the global situation is distressing as it is characterized by the "multitudes of the hungry, the needy, the homeless, those without medical care, and above all those without hope of a better future."[66] With these situations, the poor are becoming poorer and the rich are becoming richer.

One important principle that governs the whole encyclical is the principle of solidarity. For John Paul II, solidarity is both a duty and virtue. To achieve authentic human development, the "logic of blocs" which hinders the initiatives for development is transformed to "logic of solidarity." Solidarity "is not a feeling of vague compassion or shallow distress at the misfortunes of so many people...[Rather] it is a form and persevering determination to commit oneself to the common good; that is to say, to the good of all and of each individual, because we are all really responsible for all"[67] Against this background, solidarity is the appropriate response to conquer the chasm between rich and poor. It is the virtue that becomes fundamental as an approach to the social ills in the international society.

Additionally, John Paul II sees the importance of *option or love of preference* for the poor. According to him, "this is an option, or special form of primacy in the exercise of Christian charity, to which the whole tradition bears witness."[68] This *love of preference* for the poor guides and inspires the moral choices and actions that are to be undertaken.

---

[64] *Populorum Progressio*, no. 3.

[65] *Populorum Progressio*, no. 47.

[66] John Paul II, Encyclical On the Social Concerns *Sollicitudo Rei Socialis:* (30 December 1987), no. 42. Prior to this encyclical, John Paul II wrote *Laborem Exercens* on December 4, 1981 to commemorate the ninetieth anniversary of Leo XIII's *Rerum Novarum.* What is central to *Laborem Exercens* is the human dignity and solidarity among workers. John Paul II's emphasis on solidarity is also evident in *Sollicitudo Rei Socialis.*

[67] *Sollicitudo Rei Socialis*, no. 39.

[68] *Sollicitudo Rei Socialis*, no. 42.

Therefore, hunger can be approached from the principles of solidarity and the preferential option for the poor.

4.13. *Caritas in Veritate*

The *Caritas in Veritate* is the third encyclical of Pope Benedict XVI promulgated in 2009 which deals with the questions on the integral human development that is characterized by charity and truth. Coming out, not long after his encyclicals on *Deus Caritas Est* (2005) and *Spe Salvi* (2007), Benedict XVI asserts that *Caritas in Veritate* (Charity in Truth) is "the principle around which the Church's social doctrine turns, a principle that takes on practical form in the criteria that governs moral action."[69] In short, charity is the prime principle behind the social teaching and social actions of the Church. Justice and the common good are the two important criteria in any forms of moral and social actions.

In his reflection on human development, he sees the harrowing problem of hunger and poverty in poor countries in which the goods of the earth are not shared equally with the victims of endemic hunger. For Benedict XVI, "feeding the hungry is an ethical imperative for the universal Church...."[70] He sees hunger as not merely the lack of material things or the condition brought about by the shortage of social resources. Rather, it is institutional. He further argues that what is missing in the whole question of hunger is "the network of economic institutions capable of guaranteeing regular access to sufficient food and water for nutritional needs, and also capable of addressing the primary needs and necessities ensuing from genuine food crises..."[71] These institutional reforms in pursuit of eliminating the structures that contribute to hunger must be taken into action in order to vouch for sustainable access to food. He concludes that "food and access to water as universal rights of all human beings, without distinction or discrimination" must be plowed into public awareness because this "right to food, like the right to water, has an important place within the pursuit of other rights."[72]

5. Assessment of the Catholic Social Teachings on Hunger

The above Magisterial documents from *Rerum Novarum* to *Caritas in Veritate* are surveyed to understand their responses to the problem of hunger. Undeniably, the Church has been interfering with the hope that this problem is eradicated. However, these documents may directly deal with the problem of hunger, but it is unfortunate that the social transformation one needs to eradicate hunger is not actualized. The documents should not remain as mere issuance of documents, but they must bring genuine transformation in the society which includes the alleviation of hunger.

---

[69] Benedict XVI, Encyclical on Charity in Truth *Caritas in Veritate* (29 June 2009), no. 6 (Paulines: Pasay, 2009).
[70] *Caritas in Veritate,* no. 27.
[71] *Caritas in Veritate,* no. 27.
[72] Caritas in Veritate, no. 27.

It is noteworthy that the Social Catholic Teachings which are mentioned above are not only intended first to the bishops but to all men and women of faith. Drawing inspiration from *Gaudium et Spes*, the Church has opened herself to the world and began to morally and pastorally discern the social problems which are continuously impinged on the life of the human fabric and of the nations. This responsive act towards the social problem is not alone the social advocacy of those who are in the hierarchy. Rather, the whole members of the Body of Christ are moved to respond to the social crises.

Finally, a critique of the social problems undertaken by the Church's Social Teachings is not anymore based on natural law ethics but on Gospel-based critique.[73] This is evident in the latter encyclicals which are more pastoral in their approach and more action-committed. In other words, the methodology is shifted from ethical principles which instruct the faithful on how to act in this world based on the natural laws to discernment based on the Gospel imperatives. So, it is no longer "right doctrine" or "right reason" but "right action."[74]

Conclusion

We have studied in this chapter the hunger situation in the Philippines. To situate hunger, we have dealt with Monika Hillwig's understanding of hunger. Then, we saw that hunger is a perennial problem in the global world. Even in first-world countries, hunger too is a social concern. Among the continents, Asia shares a big chunk of the whole spectrum of hunger due to its population. The Philippines as an Asian country is also exposed to hunger and malnutrition. We have seen the various causes of this hunger like natural calamities, poverty, corruption, and military conflict.

We have seen how the non-government organizations and other institutions contribute to the eradication of hunger. The concerted efforts of these institutions have helped in mitigating hunger. Then, we saw that the Philippine government is also concerned about hunger. We have identified some of the government policies and programs as a response to this social problem. The Philippine Church too plays a significant role in this effort to end hunger.

---

[73] Francisco Javier, *The Making of a Local Church* (Quezon City: Claretian Publication, 2009), 75.
[74] Ibid., 75.

CHAPTER 2

A Survey of the Biblical, Historical and Theological Development of the Rite of the Presentation of the Gifts

In the Eucharistic liturgy prior to the Second Vatican Council, the rite has a different name which is known as "Offertory" in the West. Once the Roman Missal of Paul VI was introduced, this part of the Mass was changed to "Preparation of the Gifts" to underscore that true offering happens in the Eucharistic Prayer. Central to this rite is "the disposition on the altar of the bread and wine that would become the Body and Blood of Christ."[75] This is the original and essential nucleus of this part of the liturgy; other rites are only added over the centuries.

This chapter explores the biblical, patristic, liturgical, and theological foundations of the rite of the presentation of the gifts. It shows that this rite has a transformative role in addressing social concerns like hunger. The connection between the act of worship and the act of justice is highlighted in this chapter. It also intends to trace the origin of the rite from Didache, Justin the Martyr, Irenaeus, Hippolytus of Rome, and Cyprian. The offertory in the West, as well as the decline of this offertory in the Middle Ages until its recovery in the Roman Missal of Paul VI, is discussed. This chapter ends on the theological themes of the rite.

1. Biblical themes on Eucharist

In the Old and New Testaments, there are no explicit or concrete references which are regarded as a sacrament. Jesus did not categorically identify that this or that is a sacrament. But the Bible is not devoid of rituals and practices which constitute the sacraments today. On this note, this section deals with some practices in the Old Testament which are significant to the sacrament of the Eucharist. In the New Testament, the public ministry of Jesus is also considered. Then, Paul's concern for the needy is discussed too.

---

[75] Robert Cabie, *The Eucharist,* ed. Aime Georges Martimort, trans. Matthew O'Connel, *The Church at Prayer 2* (Collegeville, MN: Liturgical Press, 1986), 78.

1.1. Old Testament

One needs to understand that the Old Testament finds its full meaning in the New while the New Testament is hidden in the Old.[76] In the same vein, the Eucharist which is not present in the Old Testament is prefigured in the Old Testament through some events and ways.[77] One cannot find the Eucharist in the Old Testament, but there are events and ways in the Old Testament which pointed to the existence of the Eucharist in the New Testament. On one occasion, Abraham, after he returned from the slaughter of Chedorlaomer, was welcomed by Melchizedek who brought offerings of bread and wine and blessed Abraham.[78] The bread and wine are sacrifices which are important substances in the Eucharist. These two elements are also present in Passover as well as manna in the desert.

Essentially, the Eucharist is characterized as a sacrifice. This act of sacrifice is a practice that is found in the Old Testament. A sacrifice is an act of dependence and conformity to the god. There are three kinds of sacrifice in the Old Testament.[79] These are communion sacrifice, gift sacrifice, and sin offering. The gift sacrifices are burnt offerings offered to God as an act of praise and thanksgiving.[80] The communion sacrifices are occasions of sharing a feast with the god.[81] Food is offered to show the union between the god and those who shared in the sacrificial meal. Next, the sin offering in which the people acknowledge their past sins against the god.[82] Through this offering, the people are purified from their sins and the mutual union between the god and the people are brought back. These three categories of sacrifices, which have been a practice by the ancient religion, have some elements of eating, sharing, and thanksgiving. Of all the instances in the Old Testament, the sacrificial offering of the first fruits is considered here.

---

[76] "God the inspirer and author of the books of both Testaments, in his wisdom has so brought it about that the New should be hidden in the Old and that the Old should be made manifest in the New." Vatican Council II, Dogmatic Constitution on Divine Revelation *Dei Verbum* (18 November 1965) no. 16, in Vatican Council II: The Conciliar and Post Conciliar Documents, ed. Austin Flannery (Pasay City: Paulines, 2006).

[77] Izunna Okonkwo, "Transformative Power of the Eucharist with Special Attention to the Harrowing Problem of Hunger: A Theological Exploration with South East Nigeria as a Point of Reference," (PhD. diss., Katholieke Universiteit Leuven, 2011), 75.

[78] Brian Pizzalato, "Eucharist Foreshadowed in Old Testament Writings," https://www.catholicnewsagency.com/resources/sacraments/eucharist/eucharist-foreshadowed-in-old-testament-writings, (accessed 21.05.18). See Gen. 14:17-24.

[79] Kenneth W. Stevenson, *Eucharist and Offering* (New York: Pueblo Publishing Company, 1986), 13.

[80] Cf. Leviticus 1.

[81] Cf. Leviticus 3 and 7.

[82] Cf. Leviticus 4-7.

1.2. Sacrificial Offering of the First Fruits in Deuteronomy 26

Moses commanded the Israelites to sacrifice the first fruits of their harvest to thank Yahweh for the abundance of harvest and gift of land.[83] Deuteronomy 26:3-10 mentions the accompanying declaration that is to be recited when the Israelites have to offer. Standing in front of the altar with the basket of the first fruits, the Israelites must utter the declaration in v. 3-10. What is striking about this declaration is when the Israelites, as they offer before the altar, remember that their "father was a wandering Aramean." Other translations use "Syrian was my father." Both are referred to Jacob and his descendants who were poor, oppressed, despised, and enslaved in Egypt. Thus, a person who offered the first fruits recognizes the nation of which he was a member and remembers the oppressed members of his origin.

Furthermore, verses 2-3 show that the gift of the first fruits of the harvest was to be placed in a basket and presented to the priest at the sanctuary. And then, the priest presented the gifts, on behalf of the people, to God. The acceptance of the gifts by the priest from the Israelites represents God's pleasure with the gift. But going further to the text, one can surmise that fruits of the harvest are also shared with the poor. Goffredo Boselli argues that Deuteronomy 26 is not only a remembrance of Yahweh's marvelous deeds to the Israelites; it is also "a memorial of the present, an appeal to Israel's responsibility in daily living."[84]

Hence, the text has an ethical demand to share the first fruits of their labor as evident in verse 11.[85] During those times, the Levites are deprived of the right to possess the land and they rely on the people's generosity to live. The Israelites, as an ethical command, must celebrate with the Levites of what they have.[86] The abundance of the land that God has gifted to the Israelites must be distributed to and enjoyed by the Levites, who were deprived of land possession. Thus, Deuteronomy 26 is concerned with marginal people in society. In fact, in the second half of the chapter, it demonstrates the purpose of the tithe. The tithe, which is reckoned after a three-year period, functioned for the upkeep of the Levites, the aliens, orphans, and widows. The economic wellbeing of these people is dependent on the Hebrew community. As cited by Boselli, Antonio Bonora claims that offering the gifts ``is not therefore the pretty and egotistical joy of the one who 'enjoys' his piece of earth, but rather the gratitude of all and of each one for a

[83] "You shall take some of the firstfruits of all that produce from the soil of the land the Lord your God is giving you and put them in a basket" Deuteronomy 26:2. This passage is similar to Deuteronomy 16:16 when the Israelites have to bring gifts to the altar and "shall not appear before the Lord empty-handed."

[84] Goffredo Boselli, *The Spiritual Meaning of the Liturgy: School of Prayer, Source of Life*, trans. Barry Hudock (Collegeville, MN: Liturgical Press, 2014), 82.

[85] "Then you, together with the Levites and the aliens who reside among you, shall celebrate with all the bounty that the Lord your God has given you and to your house." Deuteronomy 26:11.

[86] Boselli, *The Spiritual Meaning of the Liturgy: School of Prayer, Source of Life*, 82.

gift to share...with the poor who lack the access to the fruits of the earth."[87] The poor too are the recipients of the presentation of the gifts.

Thus, when the Israelites offered their first fruits from the harvest, they earnestly abandoned their self-centeredness and complete monopoly of the goods. Worship and thanksgiving to the Lord become complete and perfect by the care for the poor. Loius-Marie Chauvet believes that "it is in the ethical practice of sharing that the liturgy of Israel is thus accomplished. The rite is the symbolic representation of the conjunction between the love of God and love of neighbor in which Israel will discern...not only the central double commandment but also the very principle of the whole Law."[88]

1.3. Matthew's Gospel: Discipleship and table sharing

Central to Matthew's Gospel are the commands of Jesus, especially the feeding of the hungry.[89] In chapter 25:31-46, Matthew sums up the theme of Jesus' identification with the poor and the hungry in the Final Judgement that concludes the pre-passion narrative. This identification with the poor and hungry is significant because it is described as a direct service to God.[90] Hospitality to the poor and welcoming the strangers constitute the conditions to inherit God's kingdom when the Final Judgement comes. Nonetheless, to inherit the kingdom is to put to an end the "oppressive systems and exploitative societal relationships, and the fair access to the necessary resources for life."[91] In fact, one sees that the kingdom of God is like a banquet or feast in which Jesus invited the sinners, the outcast and the socially excluded to share in the banquet table of the kingdom. This invitation of Jesus to eat with him breaks the social divisions which is a sign of the coming of the reign of God. If the faithful are true disciples of Christ, then they must do exactly what he did to the socially excluded members of the society.

The basis on which judgment is made is on one's relationship with the neighbor. But the love of neighbor is more than just an act; it is in fact, a significant dimension of discipleship because Jesus himself shows great affection and love towards the poor. So, the people are judged not purely in terms of their relationship with the needy but on how they carry out their call of discipleship and undertake the values of the Good News.[92] One is judged according to his/her response to the call of discipleship. For St. Jerome, "I was hungry, and you gave me something to eat" presents "a practical religion of deeds of loving-kindness... (which) is addressed to Christian disciples, and discipleship is

---

[87] Boselli, *The Spiritual Meaning of the Liturgy: School of Prayer, Source of Life*, 83. Cited in Antonio Bonora, "Dalla storia e dalla natura alla professione de fede e alla celebrazione (Deut 26:1-15)," Parola, Spirito, e Vita 25 (1992): 29.

[88] Louis-Marie Chauvet, *Symbol and Sacrament: A Sacramental Reinterpretation of Christian Existence* (Collegeville, MN: Liturgical Press, 1995), 238.

[89] Joseph Grassi, *Broken Bread and Broken Bodies: The Lord's Supper and World Hunger* (New York: Orbis Books, 1985), 56.

[90] Ibid., 35.

[91] Warren Carter, *Matthew and the Margins: A Sociopolitical and Religious Reading* (Maryknoll, New York: Orbis Books, 2000), 494.

[92] Carter, *Matthew and the Margins: A Sociopolitical and Religious Reading*, 492.

understood in a very bold way as identical with care of the needy."[93] This text is much concerned about the call of discipleship. As disciples of Jesus, they must use their resources to respond to the needs of the hungry and participate in all efforts to break the walls between the rich and the poor. Thus, Joseph Grassi, argues that "discipleship is closely connected with the hungry."[94]

1.4. Luke's Gospel: Service and table sharing

In the Synoptic Gospels, feeding the hungry is central to the ministry of Jesus as he commanded his disciples: "You yourselves give them to eat."[95] For instance in Luke 1:53, Mary, in her gladness of thanksgiving, proclaims: "to the hungry he has given every good thing." Or, in Luke's version of the Sermon on the Mount, Jesus promises that blessings are assured to the hungry: "Blessed are you who are hungry now; you shall be satisfied."[96] In here Luke stresses the blessing contrary to verse 25 in which he underscores the curse: "Woe to you who are satisfied, for you will be hungry." Regardless of the emphasis between these two versions, Luke is pointing out that those who are hungry must be provided with bread to eat. This is similar to Luke's version of the Lord's prayer in which bread is given to the hungry: "Give us each day our daily bread."[97]

Furthermore, Luke's table sharing relates to service. In Luke's account of the Lord's Supper, the disciples are discussing who should be regarded as the greatest among them. Jesus responded that the greatest among them are those who take the role of servant and become the least. Jesus' answer implies that to be true disciples of Jesus they must serve the *least, the last and the lost* in the community- the poor, oppressed and the hungry. These people in the community are the guests who are invited to the banquet and thus share a common meal. Luke too places the theme on table fellowship of Jesus in which the outcast, the poor, the strangers, sinners and the lowly are to be welcomed at God's banquet and take honored seats in the common tables. The disciples must be hospitable to them, be friends with them and serve them. Loving service to the poor includes welcoming them in the Lord's banquet.

1.5. Acts of the Apostles: Living a common life

In the Acts of the Apostles, it describes how the Christian communities live together and share their possessions with one another.

[93] Raymond E. Brown, Joseph A. Fitzmyer, Roland E. Murphy eds., *The New Jerome Biblical Commentary*, with a foreword by Carlo Maria Cardinal Martini, SJ (Bangalore Theological Publications in India: Bangalore, 2013), 669.

[94] Grassi, *Broken Bread and Broken Bodies: The Lord's Supper and World Hunger*, 59.

[95] Cf., Matthew 14:16; Mark 6:37; Luke 9:13

[96] Luke 6:21

[97] Luke 11:3.

> Now they were persevering in the doctrine of the Apostles, and in the communion of the breaking of the bread, and in the prayers. And fear developed in every soul. Also, many miracles and signs were accomplished by the Apostles in Jerusalem. And there was a great awe in everyone. And then all who believed were together, and they held all things in common. Also, they continued, daily, to be of one accord in the temple and to break bread among the houses; and they took their meals with exultation and simplicity of heart, and praising God greatly, and holding favour with all the people. And every day, the Lord increased those who were being saved among them.[98]

The early Christians would sell their property and possessions and share them with the community. The breaking of the bread took place in private houses, and they joyfully ate their meals with others. Thus, the life of the early Christian communities is characterized by sharing their goods which are deeply rooted in the breaking of the bread. The Eucharist is therefore related to communion and fellowship.

1.6. New Testament Epistles: Meal-sharing in Paul's Epistles

During the time of Paul, common meals and living equally as one community are the descriptions that best understand the life of early Christian communities. They share one bread and one eucharistic cup. This characteristic of the Christians as koinonia does not only apply in the Eucharistic table-sharing but also in social relationships.[99] It is not a characteristic of koinonia when the Christians gathered for the eucharist and yet the poor members of the community are denied food. Poverty is not also a character of the Christian community. All must be in solidarity with the poor in combating poverty in the community. To respond to poverty, Paul made collections from the prosperous church in Corinth for the needy in the Jerusalem church.[100] Whoever is in need, the other churches should share.

But Paul is frustrated with the Christians in Corinth when he found out that the division between the rich and the poor who share the common meal is worsening. Paul writes:

> "When you assemble it is not to eat the Lord's Supper, for everyone is in haste to eat his own support. One person is hungry while another gets

---

[98] Acts of the Apostles 2:42-47.

[99] William R. Crockett, *Eucharist: Symbol of Transformation* (New York: Pueblo Publishing Company, 1989), 254.

[100] Cf. 1 Corinthians 16:1-4.

> drunk...Would you show contempt for the Church of God and embarrass those who have nothing."[101]

Paul, therefore, is reminding the Christians to show some concern to the poor, the members of the Body of Christ, as they share in Christ's body in the Last Supper. His view on being a member of Christ's Body implies a distinct responsibility to manifest love and compassion towards others. He can establish a link between the Eucharist and care for the needy. For instance, the collection on Sunday is shared with people in need. The purpose of this collection is for "fellowship and equality based on sharing."[102] He says:

> "About the collection for the saints, follow the instructions I gave to the churches of Galatia. On the first day of each week, everyone should put aside whatever he has been able to save so that the collection will not have to be taken up after I arrive."[103]

Since the time of the Apostles, social consciousness related to the breaking of bread is very much alive in the Christian communities. The breaking of the bread is so powerful that it impacted the socialism of the Christians. Even in the early liturgies, social consciousness has gained its significant character as the liturgy highlights its social dimension. For instance, in the offering of the gifts, its social dimension is appreciated in caring for the needy. In the early liturgies, there is indeed a close relationship between the "offering of the gifts and the care for the needy."[104]

1.7. Didache

The Didache is the earliest account that describes the celebration of the Eucharist which can be traced back to the end of the first century.[105] It notes in Chapter 14:

> On the Lord's own day, assemble in common to break bread and offer thanks, but first, confess your sins so that your sacrifice may be pure. However, no one quarreling with his brother may join your meeting until they are reconciled; your sacrifice must not be defiled. For here we have the saying of the Lord: "In every place and time offer me a pure sacrifice; for I

---

[101] Cf. 1 Corinthians 11:20-22.

[102] Grassi, *Broken Bread and Broken Bodies: The Lord's Supper and World Hunger*, 88.

[103] 1 Corinthians 16:11.

[104] Crockett, *Eucharist: Symbol of Transformation,* 254.

[105] The Didache contains the doctrine of the Twelve Apostles which was rediscovered by Bryennios in 1873. It is divided into three parts: the first part is the "Two Ways," the Way of Life and the Way of Death; the second part includes the rituale of baptism, fasting and Holy Communion; and the third part deals with the ministry. For a complete text, see John Chapman, *Didache,* The Catholic Encyclopedia, Vol. 4 (New York: Robert Appleton Company, 1908).

> am a mighty king, says the Lord; and my name spreads terror among the nations.[106]

What is important in this passage is the understanding of the Eucharist as sacrifice. But this concept of sacrifice does not refer to the rite but to the gift offered.[107] The gifts offered are not the same as the sacrifice like Jews and pagan cults. Rather, it is a sacrifice that must be "pure and undefiled."[108]

Furthermore, *Didache* describes these gifts offered are meant for the prophet and the poor:

> Take all the first-fruits of the winepress and of the harvest, of the cattle and of the sheep, and given them to the prophets, for they are your high priests. But, if you have not a prophet, give it to the poor. If you make bread, take the first share, and give according to the commandment (13:3-5)[109]

The celebration of the Eucharist is characterized as thanksgiving to the Father in the memory of Jesus' death and resurrection. The bread and wine are called Eucharist because they are transformed into the Body and Blood of Christ.[110] The Christians too have an active role in the sacrifice of thanksgiving. The bringing of bread and wine are the expression of their communion in the eucharistic community as well as the contribution to the needy. Here the social significance of offering is predominant during this time.

2. Historical Development of the Presentation of the Gifts

After establishing the link between Eucharist and care for the needy, the next part deals with the historical development of the presentation of the gifts and its possible connection with hunger. At this juncture, the Fathers of the Church as well as the development of the rite, are considered.

2.1. Development of Sacrificial Offering in the Early Church from First to Third Century

The Fathers of the Church are influential theologians who are not considered the apostles of Jesus, but they have significant contributions to the Church's theology. Through their knowledge and understanding, the theology of the Eucharist was developed. Here, the focus is on the theology of the Eucharist and its relationship with

---

[106] Michael McGuckian, *The Holy Sacrifice of the Mass,* (Chicago: Liturgy Training Publications, 2005), 57.

[107] Ibid., 57.

[108] Cf. Mal. 1:11.

[109] Grassi, *Broken Bread and Broken Bodies: The Lord's Supper and World Hunger*, 90.

[110] Edward J. Kilmartin, SJ, "The Sacrifice of Thanksgiving and Social Justice," in *Liturgy and Social Justice*, ed. Mark Searle (Collegeville, MN: Liturgical Press, 1980), 57.

social justice with special interest on the problem of hunger. To substantiate this relationship, other sources which contain significant descriptions of Eucharistic celebrations are considered.

2.1.1. Justin the Martyr

The *Apologia* of Justin the Martyr contains the "first concrete description of the Eucharist celebration."[111] His first account contains a description on the Eucharistic celebration while the second account concerns the Sunday Mass. Significant in Justin's Eucharistic theology is his understanding of Sunday as the special day for Eucharistic celebration. He describes this gathering as follows:

> But we all hold this common gathering on Sunday since it is the first day, on which God transforming darkness and matter made the Universe, and Jesus Christ our Saviour on the same day rose from the dead. For they crucified Him on the day before Saturday, and on the day after Saturday, He appeared to His Apostles and disciples and taught them these things which we have passed on to you also for your consideration.[112]

As regards with the description of the offertory procession of the faithful on Sunday gathering, Justin did not give the full account. The bread and wine mixed with water are simply brought in and are placed on the table before the beginning of ceremonies. Jungmann describes it as "no particular formalities observed, no symbolism introduced in the movement."[113] The preparation of bread and wine is not a "ritual action."[114] The Church during this time has greatly emphasized the spiritual nature of the Christian cult as opposed to the Jewish sacrificial customs. "The Church's attention focused on the spiritual, not to say heavenly, gift which proceeds from her *Eucharistia,* and on the thanksgiving which pours out heavenward from the hearts of men-worship which is indeed "in spirit and in truth."[115]

But this Sunday gathering has a social dimension as the poor and widows are remembered in the celebration. He stresses that the Sunday liturgy promotes equality between the rich and the poor through sharing that takes in the common meal. He added that after the Sunday gathering, the president distributes to the widows, the orphans, the

---

[111] Joseph A. Jungmann, SJ, *The Mass* (Collegeville, Minnesota: The Liturgical Press, 1976), 24.

[112] Walter J. Burghardt, John J. Dillon, Dennis D. McManus, eds., *Ancient Christian Writers: The Works of Fathers* in Translation no. 56 St. Justin Martyr: The First and Second Apologies trans. Leslie William Barnard, no. 67, 71-72.

[113] Joseph Jungmann, SJ, *The Mass of the Roman Rite: Its Origins and Development,* trans. Francis A. Brunner (London: Burns and Oats, 1959), 315.

[114] Ibid., 315.

[115] Ibid.,315.

sick and the imprisoned what has been collected from the wealthy during the Eucharistic sacrifice.[116] He urges the rich to contribute to the welfare of the poor. He contends:

> The wealthy, if they wish, contribute whatever they desire, and the collection is placed in the custody of the president. With it he helps the orphans and widows, those who are needy because of sickness or any other reason, he takes care of all those in need (Chap. 67).[117]

The wealthy people must extend their help to the widows and the orphans and the needy in the community. They must come to the aid of the poor and exhibit sensibilities toward them. The alms collected are "in place of the custody of the president" who takes care of the widows and the orphans. Although the rite of presentation of the gifts is never mentioned in his treatises, it is noteworthy to affirm that to collect the gifts for the poor is a "liturgical act" and the president of the community's Eucharistic offering takes the responsibility to share them to the poor.[118] Here, the Church's celebration of the Eucharist goes beyond the physical community and extends to the absent members of the community as manifested by the collection of alms for the needy. The Eucharist has some link with sharing the earthly possessions.

Hence, Justin "developed a Eucharistic theology that not only emphasized the communitarian character of the Eucharist but also a unique concern for the less privileged."[119] Such thought brings one to interpret the theology of the Eucharist as not purely bound by rubricist mentality but as a celebration which needs to be transformed in the human experience of the people with the utmost attention to the needy and the poor.

2.1.2. St. Irenaeus

St. Irenaeus was interested too in the Eucharist. Here, the Eucharist takes a different light. Unlike Justin, he emphasizes the material dimension of the Eucharist as the "firstlings of creation" are offered.[120] In his fourth book of his treatise "Against the Heresies," Irenaeus claims that Jesus commanded his apostles "offer up to God the firstlings of all creation, not because he needs these things, but that they themselves may not appear barren and ungrateful"[121] when he took the bread and the chalice during the Last Supper. From this phrase, two important points need to be undertaken. First, God

[116] Justin Martyr, "First Apology Chapter 65," in *The Catholic Tradition: Mass and the Sacraments* Vol. 1, , ed. Charles J. Dollen, et al, (America: Mc Grath Publishing Company, 1979), 29.

[117] Grassi, *Broken Bread and Broken Bodies: The Lord's Supper and World Hunger,* 90.

[118] Boselli, *The Spiritual Meaning of the Liturgy: School of Prayer, Source of Life*, 88.

[119] Izunna Okonkwo, "Transformative Power of the Eucharist with Special Attention to the Harrowing Problem of Hunger: A Theological Exploration with Southeast Nigeria as a Point of Reference," (PhD. diss., Katholieke Universiteit Leuven, 2011), 105.

[120] Jungmann, *The Mass,* 186.

[121] Ibid., 28.

does not need these sacrifices. But the faithful become ungrateful if they fail to present the gifts. These gifts must be offered "in purity and innocence...for sacrifices cleanse not the man but the offerer's conscience makes the sacrifice hold."[122] Second, the sacrifice offered must come from the firstlings of creation.

His emphasis on the material element of the Eucharist is actually a response to the Gnostics of his time whose orientation is anti-matter. He defended the goodness of materialism over spiritualism. Therefore, Irenaeus' contribution to the Eucharist is the inclusion of the presentation of the material gifts for the offering up to God which are drawn into the liturgical activity.

2.1.3. Hippolytus of Rome

Hippolytus of Rome, a Roman presbyter, and writer during the third century, is significant in the whole understanding of the Eucharist contained in the *Traditio Apostolica.* In his Church Ordinance, he speaks about the offertory of the people during Eucharistic Sacrifice. But Hippolytus never mentions about an offertory procession.[123] He said that "everyone should be mindful to offer to the bishop the firstfruits of the field."[124] He further notes:

> These are the fruits which are to be blessed: grapes, figs, apples, olives, pears, pomegranates, peaches, cherries, and almonds; but lotus, onions, garlic, pumpkins, cucumbers, and other vegetables are not to be blessed. If flowers are brought, the roses and lilies are to be accepted; others should be rejected.[125]

He made a clear distinction between those which are acceptable and unacceptable for the celebration. Although it is not clear on how these gifts were offered to the altar, what is certain is that there is indeed the presentation of the gifts during his time. Interestingly, the words *offerre* and *oblatio* are used not only in reference to the Eucharistic gifts but in reference to the bread and the cup shared in the community. The bread and wine are taken as oblations prior to Eucharistic prayer.

2.1.4. Cyprian

St. Cyprian's understanding of the Eucharist can be deduced from his Letter 63 to Caecilius. *Offerre, oblation* or *sacrificium* are now accepted as terms associated with the

---

[122] Ibid., 28.

[123] Pius Parsch, *The Liturgy of the Mass,* trans. Rev. Frederick C. Eckhoff, (London: B Herder Book Co, 1942), 155.

[124] Ibid., 155.

[125] Ibid., 156.

Eucharist.[126] This Eucharistic celebration is called *sacrificium Dominicum* (Lord's sacrifice) or simply *dominicum* due to the fact that "at the Last Supper Christ made the offering and even now continues to make it through the priest."[127] Christ as the High Priest offered himself to the Father as a sacrificial victim so that sins are washed out. "As Christ has borne our sins by his sufferings, so too in this sacrifice the people are joined to Christ just as inseparable as the water to the wine."[128] The faithful share in the sacrifice of Christ and thus become gifts offered to God. In other words, the Christian people have active participation in the sacrifice of Christ.

Connected to this active participation is to contribute bread and wine for the celebration. It is also to give alms to the poor. He reprimands those "who come without alms and in communion receive part of the sacrifice that a poor has brought."[129] Seemingly, Cyprian's attitude towards the rich woman for failing to bring gifts is indeed a manifestation that the faithful should present gifts during Eucharistic celebration. He notes:

> You are rich and wealthy and imagine that you celebrate the Lord's Supper without taking part in the offering. You come to the Lord's house with nothing to offer, suppressing the part of the sacrifice which belongs to the poor.[130]

From the Church Fathers during the first and third centuries, there are some various observations. First, their presentation of the bread and wine are not a ritual action from the beginning because of the stress on thanksgiving over the material gifts. Second, there is a shift from spiritual to the material element of the Eucharist. The value of earthly creation is underscored during the first century. Third, the presentation of the gifts became a regular course in the Eucharistic celebration only after the shift. It became a norm that the faithful should offer their gifts at Eucharistic celebration. Fourth, the Eucharist is seen as the celebration of praise and thanksgiving. The offerings are expressions of communion in the worshipping community and are considered as thank-offering to God. Fifth, the offerings are meant for the Church and for the poor which became customary.

Kilmartin argues that "the meaning attached to the presentation of the gifts at the Eucharist is determined by the basic idea that governs the understanding of the Eucharist in any given period."[131] During the first three centuries, the Eucharist is viewed as a

---

[126] Jungmann, *The Mass,* 40.

[127] Ibid., 40.

[128] Ibid., 40.

[129] Cyprian, De opera et eleemosyna, no. 15, cited by Pius Parsch, *The Liturgy of the Mass,* tr. Rev. Frederick C. Eckhoff (London: B Herder Book Co, 1942), 156.

[130] Grassi, *Broken Bread and Broken Bodies: The Lord's Supper and World Hunger*, 91.

[131] Edward J. Kilmartin, "The Sacrifice of Thanksgiving and Social Justice," in Mark Seale (ed.) *Liturgy and Social Justice,* (Collegeville, MN: Liturgical Press, 1980), 58.

"celebration of praise and thanksgiving."[132] Hence, the gifts offered in the Eucharist are the expression of praise and thanksgiving to God. The gifts offered are not meant to ask for favors from God but an expression of fellowship in the community as well as an act of thanksgiving to God. In other words, the social and collective dimension of offering the gifts is dominant in the public worship of the people in the early church. The people share in the Eucharistic bread as an expression of their Christian fellowship with God and with other Christians. It is an event where people share with those who are in need and at the same time an expression of active participation in the worship. Hence, the close relationship between public worship and social justice is expressed in the offering of gifts.

2.2. Development of Offertory in the Western Liturgy

One observes that there are various shifts in the Roman liturgy during the fourth and seventh centuries. Among these shifts is first the movement from house setting to the Constantinian Basilicas where the celebrations of the Eucharist took place. Second, the Roman liturgy is characterized by simplicity, practicality, spontaneity, intimacy, and hospitality. Third, the Roman liturgy is based on imperial court ceremonies, thus, it has characters that are solemn, ceremonial, impersonal and flamboyant. This gives birth to liturgical books of the Roman Mass that become the basis for the actions performed.

In Africa and in Rome, the Eucharistic liturgy begins with the procession of the offerers like the procession during communion.[133] The offerers approached the bishop and his ministers and gave them the offerings while a psalm was sung. A detailed description of the presentation of the gifts can be found in *Ordo Romanus Primus*. The *Ordo Romanus Primus* describes the presentation of the gifts that happen during Mass.[134] The deacon proceeds to the altar after reading the Gospel to receive the chalice and corporal from the acolyte.[135] The Pontiff accompanied by his assistants proceeded to the *senatorium* where the senators and the nobility are seated, and there he receives the offerings of the laity. The Pontiff received the offerings of bread of the nobility and the archdeacon who followed him accepted the wine. Likewise, the Pontiff handed the bread to the subdeacon who placed them in a large cloth called *sindon* carried by two acolytes. One of the bishops assisted by the deacon collected the offerings while the pontiff received the offerings from the higher court officials and ladies of nobility. The archdeacon prepares the bread offerings on the altar with the help of the assisting deacons. The Pontiff proceeded to his seat and washed his hand. His own offering is

[132] Ibid., 58.

[133] Robert Cabie, *The Eucharist,* ed. Aime Georges Martimort, trans. Matthew O'Connel, *The Church at Prayer 2* (Collegeville, MN: Liturgical Press, 1986),78.

[134] The *Ordo Romanus Primus* compiled during the seventh century contains the rubrics for the papal stational services.

[135] Michael Witczak, "History of the Latin Text and Rite," in *Commentary on the Order of Mass of the Roman Missal*, ed. Edward Foley (Quezon City: Claretian Publication, 2012), 201-209.

placed on the altar by the archdeacon.[136] Jungmann insists that not all bread and wine collected were used for the sacrifice, other gifts were placed on side altars as an oblation and set aside for the poor which are distributed by the deacons.[137]

Turning to the developments of the offering of the gifts towards the end of the third century, it is good to know that the East influenced the West as regards to this practice. As affirmed by Jungmann, the Offertory procession in Gaul came from the Byzantine solemn offertory procession which was only adapted by Rome on great certain feasts.[138] The Roman liturgy was introduced in Gallo-Frankish territory and the Offertory became a rite.

The Gallican liturgy is influenced by the Byzantine Rite. In the East, the people bring their offerings to the sacristy before the celebration begins; these gifts are brought to the altar by the deacons at the beginning of the Eucharistic liturgy.[139] This practice is also present in the Gallican liturgy. In the Gallican Mass, the Eucharistic celebration includes the second solemn procession in which the priest carries the offering or gifts to the altar.[140] But these gifts are placed to the sacristy before the Mass. The solemn procession is called the entrance of the triumphant Christ which is accompanied by the singing of hymn called *sonus.*[141] This act became a directive of the Synod of Macon which decreed that both man and woman should bring bread and wine every Sunday for the altar.[142] It also instructed the people to bring gifts "in order that they may be freed of the burden of their sins."[143] Gregory of Tours relates a story in which a woman makes an offering for her deceased husband.[144] She brings a Gaza wine to the sacristy as the start of the Mass. St. Augustine narrates that Monica, his mother, would bring the offerings to the altar every day.[145] His mother would not let the day pass without offering to the altar. Agustine illustrates:

> So constant in alms-deeds, so gracious and attentive to thy saints, not permitting one day to pass without oblation at thy altar, twice a day, morning, and evening, coming to thy Church without intermission...interceding for the salvation of her son.[146]

---

[136] Jungmann, SJ, *The Mass of the Roman Rite: Its Origins and Development,* 319. See also Michael Witczak, "History of the Latin Text and Rite," 203.

[137] Jungmann, SJ, *The Mass of the Roman Rite: Its Origins and Development,* 318.

[138] Jungmann, SJ, *The Mass of the Roman Rite: Its Origins and Development,* 324.

[139] Gregory Dix, *The Shape of the Liturgy,* (London: New York, 1945), 120.

[140] Jungmann, SJ, *The Mass of the Roman Rite: Its Origins and Development,* 36.

[141] Ibid., 36.

[142] Parsch, *The Liturgy of the Mass,* 157.

[143] *Concilium* Matisconense (548), can. 4, ed. C. De Clercq, *Concilia Galliae* (CCL 148A), 240-41.

[144] Gregory of Tours, *Liber miraculorum in Gloria confessorum,* 64, ed. B. Krusch (MGH, Script. Aev. Merov.) 1 (1885) 785-86.

[145] Jungmann, SJ, *The Mass of the Roman Rite: Its Origins and Development,* 317.

[146] Confessions, bk. V, ch. 9, no. 2.

Moreover, people bring gifts to share in the fruits of the Eucharist. In other words, the Eucharist is viewed as "a privileged place where personal concerns obtain a special hearing before God."[147] During the fourth and fifth centuries, the Roman offertory procession is characterized by "not only as a way of expressing active participation in the Eucharistic sacrifice but also as a means of obtaining for oneself through inclusion by remembrance or petition."[148] The contribution of bread and wine is not only an expression of fraternal sharing but it is also an individualized action in exchange for individual concerns. In the early Church, the offering of bread and wine was a communal act, yet this act became individualistic in the West.

A change from communal act to individualism is brought about by the personalized intentions of the offerers and the reading of their names. The people must pay the priest in the form of a stipend for a Mass. This is manifested in "the reading of the diptychs with the names of those who are offering the sacrifice, or for whom the sacrifice is being offered in a particular way" and the priest recites the prayer "after names."[149] Names and petitions of the donors are included in the liturgy. In the offering of gifts St. Jerome is dismayed regarding this practice:

> Nowadays they read out the names of those who make an offering. Thus, the Eucharist that is the ransom of sinners turns into praise of these people; they forget the widow of the gospel whose gift of two small coins to the treasury outweighed the offerings of the rich.[150]

What theology of the Eucharist that is developed in the West is that the Eucharist is "a unified act accomplished by the priest as representative of the people and as a significant means of obtaining certain favors for the living and the dead."[151] Kilmartin further explains that "the donor could be understood as co-offering in the Mass in a special way through the gift, with and through the priest, even when the gift no longer served the communitarian function of the old offertory procession."[152] The offering is induced by individualistic interests apart from the communal interest. Added to the evidence of individualistic interest is the celebration of the Mass in private houses or chapels for a particular intention. So, offering becomes an individualistic expression rather than a communal expression. This is the development that takes place from the sixth to the ninth century. The Eucharist is a unified act in which the priest is the representative of the people and the people co-offered with him; the gift of the whole

---

[147] Kilmartin, "The Sacrifice of Thanksgiving and Social Justice," 59.

[148] Kilmartin, "The Sacrifice of Thanksgiving and Social Justice," 59.

[149] Jungmann, SJ, *The Mass of the Roman Rite: Its Origins and Development,* 36.

[150] St Jerome, *In Hieremim Prophetam II*, 108, ed. S. Reiter (CCL 74; Turnhout: Brepols, 1960), 116; *idem, In Hezechielem Prophetam* VI, 16, ed. F. Glorie (CCL 75; Yurnhout: Brepols, 1964), 238. See also: Robert Cabie, *The Eucharist,* ed. Aime Georges Martimort, trans. Matthew O'Connel, *The Church at Prayer 2* (Collegeville, MN: Liturgical Press, 1986), 81.

[151] Kilmartin, "The Sacrifice of Thanksgiving and Social Justice," 59.

[152] Edward Kilmartin, The Eucharist in the West: History and Theology, ed. Robert J. Daly (Collegeville, MN: The Liturgical Press, 1998), 112.

people is offered through the hands of the priest.[153] The Roman New Missal expresses this assertion today when the priest says: "Pray, brethren, that our sacrifice may be acceptable to God, the almighty Father." The concept of co-offering of the whole community with the priest is developed and the social dimension of the offering is diminishing. The absence of the social dimension of offering makes this act individualistic.

Changes in the development of the presentation of the gifts occurred when Germanic people influenced the concept of the offering.[154] James Russel calls it "Germanization of early medieval Christianity."[155] The Germanic law develops a recompense for a gift. This is to say that every gift given to the church, or the priest is expected to have recompensed in return. Kilmartin explains that the early view of the offering is "the old Roman notion of gift giving which does not entail reciprocity. Gifts freely given are freely received without obligation of recompense."[156] In short, the priest is not obligated to recompense the donor's intentions. However, the Germanic law obligates the priest to remember in the priest's prayer of petition or Mass the donor's intentions. He is obliged to say the Mass for an exclusive and individualistic intention. From this sort of development in the offertory, what is emerged as a problem is that the gifts:

> were no longer transacted out of the fullness of the Eucharistic *koinonia* in the body of Christ, but rather made to gain access to Eucharistic realities extrinsic to the self-definition of Christian believers. The priest was increasingly seen as the mediator of this access, as having power over the blessings of the Eucharist.[157]

The contribution of bread and wine as fraternal sharing by the faithful is dramatically changed to reciprocity and exclusivity of the Eucharist. The priest becomes the mediator between God and the people; he becomes the dispenser of the blessings and graces of the Eucharist. Such exclusivism in offerings values the Mass as a place for individual intercession and blessing. The communitarian aspect of the Mass is changed to individualism and subjectivism. In effect, the gifts offered in the Mass for the support of the poor have not given special meaning; what has been heightened is the offering of the faithful as means of obtaining special favour from the priest. The Mass is not viewed as an act of thanksgiving before God; it becomes an exclusive domain of the priest to offer the intentions of the donor.

---

[153] Liber officialis III, 19, 4, 17, 36, in J. M. Hanssens, *Amalarii episcope opera liturgia omnia,* Studi e Testi 139 (Vatican City, 1948) 2:312, 316, 332).

[154] Kilmartin, "The Sacrifice of Thanksgiving and Social Justice," 60.

[155] James C. Russell, *The Germanization of Early Medieval Christiantianity: A Sociohistorical Approach to Religious Transformation* (New York: Oxford University, 1994), 212.

[156] Kilmartin, *Eucharist in the West,* 112.

[157] Francis M. Mannion, "Stipends and Eucharistic Praxis," Worship 57, no. 3 (May 1983): 194-214, 200.

One can conclude that during the seventh century, the presentation of the gifts has become an expression of people's participation in the Eucharistic celebration. The Christians greatly participate in the celebration because they "become conscious of what it means to be a celebrating community with outreach to those in need."[158] They too "express this consciousness in its central act of worship."[159] In other words, the presentation of the gifts has emerged as an important rite that is infused in the Christian worship of the people. But this consciousness weakened during the Middle Ages.

2.3. Decline of the Offertory in the Middle Ages from Eight to Fifteen Century

One major decline of the liturgy during the eight and twelve centuries is the decline in people's participation in the liturgy. The causes of the said decline are the use of Latin language in the liturgy where people do not understand the rites, the establishment of communion rails which separate the priest and the people, the climate of rubrics that treats the liturgy as a celebration to be done with strict accordance to Rubrics, and private mass. In effect, the active participation of the faithful gradually ceased.[160]

In terms of the Offertory at Mass in the West, there are factors that contributed to its decline. One of which is the use of unleavened bread in the celebration baked by the priests which became general in the West in the eleventh century.[161] Monks in the monasteries baked the bread for the Mass. The bread baked by the faithful at home and offered in the Mass is no longer usable. The people could no longer bring bread from home to offer at Mass. Leo Hay argues that "the direct connection was lost between bread and wine presented by the people and the consecrated gifts in which Christ comes to us as the Bread of eternal life."[162]

Another factor is the development of private Mass which weakened the people's participation in the Mass. Private Mass is a Mass celebrated by the priest for a few people. The Eucharist is not viewed as "the action of the people but rather of God through the intermediary of the priest."[163] The people replaced the gifts offered in the Eucharist with Mass stipend.[164] Private prayers recited silently by the priest during the presentation of the gifts also existed. More and more celebrations of private Mass are very common in the monasteries.[165] The use of the Latin language in the text of prayers and rites contributes to the decline of participation of the faithful in the celebration of the Eucharist. Consequently, the role of the worshipping community has diminished, and the

---

[158] Leo Hay, *Eucharist: A Thanksgiving Celebration* (Washington Daleware: Michael Glazier, 1989), 37.
[159] Ibid., 37.
[160] Ibid.,37.
[161] Cabie, *The Eucharist,* 132.
[162] Hay, *Eucharist: A Thanksgiving Celebration,* 38.
[163] Tissa Balasuriya, *The Eucharist and Human Liberation* (New York: Orbis Books, 1979), 29.

[164] Theodor Klauser, *A Short History of the Western Liturgy* (Oxford: Oxford University Press, 1979), 110.
[165] Michael McGuckian, *The Holy Sacrifice of the Mass* (Chicago: Liturgy Training Publications, 2005), 67.

Mass has become the priest's celebration. Robert Cabié argues that all these factors turned "the laity into onlookers so passive that the liturgical books no longer even mentioned their presence."[166] Leo Hay notes that "the role of the priest...is now seen as that of celebrant for a community which assists at his celebration. The priest is seen as offering for the people."[167] Pius Parsch describes that "the Offertory has become a purely priestly liturgy."[168] In effect, the decline of offertory led to the decline of its social dimension. No significant changes in the presentation of the gifts until the liturgical reform which followed the Second Vatican Council.

2.4. Decline of people's participation in the liturgy in the Philippine Church

The clericalization and privatization of the liturgy are evidential too in the Philippine Church. Women silently prayed the rosary while men stepped out during homily because they could not take part in the celebration. The Roman liturgy is celebrated in Latin. The texts, rites, and prayers are in Latin which weakened the liturgical communication between the Roman liturgy and the Filipinos. The language of the Roman liturgy is completely alien to the Filipinos which results in inactive participation in the liturgical celebration. The Filipinos do not understand the Latin language. The priest recites the prayers silently. The active engagement between the faithful and the priest is poor because the priest celebrates the Mass without facing the people. The people's active participation in the liturgy is not greatly underscored because of the form of worship available during that time. Translations of liturgical prayers and readings in vernacular languages in Vatican II Reform pave the way to the active participation of the faithful. The Constitution on the Liturgy says, *"in instauranda et fovenda sacra Liturgia, [actuosa participation] summopere est attendenda."*[169] This is the charter of the Constitution as evidential in the New Order of the Mass.

2.5. Reformation of the Offertory in the New Order of the Mass

Before the promulgation of the Order of Mass in 1969, it took five years of the process for the completion of the New Order of the Mass. The Project of 1964: *Specimen provisorium,* as described by Frederick McManus, has this to say:

> The priest's reception of the gifts from the people is mentioned but is not described...Standing at the centre of the altar, the priest first receives and then reverently holds the cup in his right hand and the vessel or plate with bread in his left (without any further or explicit gesture of offering). Before placing the vessels ceremonially upon the altar, he says a single formula: "As

---

[166] Cabie, *The Eucharist,* 139.

[167] Hay, *Eucharist: A Thanksgiving Celebration,* 38.

[168] Parsch, *The Liturgy of the Mass,* 165.

[169] Reform and promotion, full and active participation, all the peoples, aim before all else, primary and indispensible source, true Christian spirit. Vatican Council II, *Sacrosanctum Concilium,* no. 14.

> this bread was scattered over the mountains and was gathered into one and as wine from many vines flowed into one, so may your Church be gathered from the ends of the earth into your kingdom. Glory to you forever." [And]...the invitation *Orate, fratres* and its response are omitted.[170]

From this description, one can deduce that the people's role is to bring forward the gifts for the Eucharist and other gifts. However, it did not describe how this role is undertaken. Also, the word "offering" is never mentioned in this text which probably gives the impression that a new theological understanding of the rite has come into place. A year after, the *First Misa normativa* of 1965 was celebrated. McManus notes that "with regards to the texts, the intent was to remove anything referring to the offering of the body and blood of Christ while changing the *elevatio* of the gifts into a solemn *depositio*."[171] Perhaps, the purpose of removing the elevation of the gifts was to give emphasis that offering takes place during Eucharistic Prayer, not during the Offertory. Regarding the gifts presented, other gifts which are not used for the Eucharist itself are received by the deacon and taken by a minister to a suitable place. It is the deacon's role to receive the people's gifts.[172]

Then, the Schema of 1966 and the 1967 Synod of Bishops were produced. In the 1967 Schema, there were other changes introduced. For instance, "where the custom exists, the priest (the deacon is not mentioned) receives the gifts from the faithful at the entrance of the chancel."[173] The altar and the gifts, except the people, are incensed. Perhaps, the inclusion of the people's participation in the offertory rite is a response to Pope Paul VI's reaction:

> The offertory seems lacking because the faithful are not allowed any part in it (even though it should be part of the Mass in which their activity is more direct and obvious)...The offertory should be given a special prominence so that the faithful (of their representatives) may exercise their special roles as offerers.[174]

In the Schema of February 1968, the active participation of faithful in the offertory rite is reinforced. In fact, the social dimension of the presentation of the gifts is highlighted too. The bringing of the gifts to the altar is strongly affirmed in the first schema of 1968:

---

170 Frederick McManus, "The Roman Order of Mass from 1964 to 1969: The Preparation of the Gifts," in *Shaping English Liturgy*, eds. Peter Finn, James M. Schellman (Washington: The Pastoral Press, 1900), 107-138.

171 Ibid., 124.

172 Ibid., 124.

173 Ibid.,124.

174 Annibale Bugnini, *The Reform of the Liturgy 1948-1975* (Collegeville: The Liturgical Press, 1990), 364.

> To foster and manifest the active participation of the faithful, it is desirable that, so far as possible, the faithful themselves- at least through some of their members- should make the presentation to the priest, by bringing forward what is necessary for the celebration of the Eucharist and bearing gifts to support the needs of the Church and the poor.[175]

In the next Schema of March 1968, it gives a stern warning about the misconception of the word "offering." While gifts are brought forward by the faithful, McManus warns that "every misconception is to be avoided: it is not a sacrifice of bread and wine or an offering of the body and blood of Christ or a consecratory epiclesis."[176] Here there is no mention of "offering." In the Schema of May 1968, the *berakah* which is recited by the priest has gained clear direction. For instance, the two formulas are said inaudibly whether there is song or none. But if there is no song, it may be said aloud. If it is said aloud, the people's acclamation may be said.[177] Notably, the major shift that is to be acknowledged from the 1570 Missal of Pius V to the Missal of Paul VI is the "active participation of the people, which had faded out in the early Middle Ages, has once again been restored."[178] This insistence on the active participation of the people brings back also the social dimension of the presentation of the gifts. In the General Instruction of the Roman Missal (2002), it says:

> The offerings are then brought forward. It is praiseworthy for the bread and wine to be presented by the faithful. They are then accepted at an appropriate place by the priest or the deacon and carried to the altar. Even though the faithful no longer bring from their own possessions the bread and wine intended for the liturgy as in the past, nevertheless the rite of carrying up the offerings still retains its power and its spiritual significance.
>
> It is also that money or other gifts for the poor or for the Church, brought by the faithful or collected in the Church, should be received. These are to be put in a suitable place but away from the Eucharistic table.

The reformed rite invites the faithful to actively participate in the procession of the gifts as a way of carrying on "the spiritual value and meaning of the ancient custom when the people brought bread and wine for the liturgy from their homes."[179] This offertory procession is a time for the faithful to show their active and conscious

---

[175] McManus, "The Roman Order of Mass from 1964 to 1969: The Preparation of the Gifts,"126

[176] Ibid., 127.

[177] Ibid., 129.

[178] McGuckian, *The Holy Sacrifice of the Mass*, 74.

[179] Rev. Annibale Bugnini, "The New *'Ordo Missae'*, *'L'Osservatore Romano,'*" May 22, 1969, 8, cited in Leo Hay, Eucharist: A Thanksgiving Celebration, (Wilmington, Delaware: Michael Glazier, 1989), 39.

participation in the celebration. At the same time, the social dimension of the rite is reinforced. The *Ordo Missae* has only this to say: "It is desirable that the participation of the faithful be expressed by members of the congregation bringing up the bread and wine for the celebration of the Eucharist or other gifts to relieve the needs of the Church and of the poor."

The Instruction also allows money and other gifts collected in the Church be offered by the faithful which are meant for the poor and for the Church. Edward Foley explains: "For this ritual to achieve such power, it is necessary for a worshipping community to have a sustained and recognizable commitment to the poor and oppressed that both extends outside of worship and also has explicitly been brought to prayer in the liturgy."[180] The Instruction's vision can only retain "its force and spiritual significance" when the poor are adequately considered.

3. Theology of the Preparation of the gifts

3.1. God as the source of all things

Robert Ledogar argues that the offertory is "thanksgiving for the gifts of creation or, better perhaps, an acknowledgment of the material universe as a gift to man."[181] Similarly, Robert Ledogar, observes that the offertory of the Mass is a rite of thanksgiving.[182] Historians agree that most of the "eucharistic prayers of the Christian traditions find their origins to the Jewish literacy and cultic form called *berakah* or blessing."[183] The prayer of blessing *(berakah)* expresses praise and thanksgiving to the many gifts God has given. Also, the word "Eucharist" comes from the Greek word *eucharisteō* which means to give thanks. It is an acknowledgment of God as the source of food and sustenance. Hellwig notes:

> a grace over meals is not in the first place a blessing of food but a blessing of God who is the source of this food and of all life and sustenance...(And) to bless God is to acknowledge him as the source of blessings, to honor him with praise and thanksgiving."[184]

---

[180] Edward Foley, "The Structure of the Mass, Its Elements and Its Parts," in *Commentary on the General Instruction of the Roman Missal*, ed. Edward Foley (Collegeville, MN: Liturgical Press, 2007), 166.

[181] Robert J. Ledogar, "The Eucharistic Prayer and the Gifts Over which It is Spoken," in *Living Bread and Saving Cup: Readings on the Eucharist,* ed. R. Kevin Seasoltz (Collegeville, Minnesota: Liturgical Press, 1982), 75.

[182] Ibid., 72.

[183] Ibid., 64.

[184] Hellwig, *The Eucharist and the Hunger of the World*, 40-41.

In the prayer, "Blessed are you, Lord, God of all creation..." one recognizes that everything comes from the "God of all creation." The gifts that come from him are signs of God's goodness, and concern to people. Thus, the response of the faithful to God's wonderful deeds is gratitude and admiration. The bread and wine are gifts the people received from God. The gifts of bread and wine offered as an oblation or offering to God before the Eucharistic prayer are offered in grateful acknowledgement to God's graciousness. Thus, Josef Jungmann notes that "before we enjoy them, we must raise them up to God and "make them free" by blessing him; we must render him thanks for them."[185] Consequently, the *berakah* pronounced over the bread and wine are prayers in thanksgiving to God's goodness and kindness. But it must be stressed that what the people offer are God's gifts and they are only stewards so that in offering him these gifts which become the expression of their self-offering and thanksgiving, they are offering him that which is already his.[186] This is affirmed in the weekday prefaces of 1970 Roman Missal:

> Father...we do well always and everywhere to give you thanks. You have no need of our praise, yet our desire to thank you is itself your gift. Our prayer of thanksgiving adds nothing to your greatness, but makes us grow in your greatness, but makes us grow in your grace, through Jesus Christ our Lord.[187]

This prayer asserts that the gifts offered by the faithful do not add to God's greatness. God does not need the gifts of the faithful. It is even more the need of the faithful to offer as they acknowledged their dependence on God. As Christians who are thankful to God, they must recognize their dependence on God the Creator but at the same time take charge of God's creation. And part of this God's creation is to take care of the people who are in hunger situations.

3.2. Communion in the Mystical Body of Christ

The Second Vatican Council gives emphasis on the active, full, and conscious participation of the faithful in the celebration of the Eucharist.[188] It is this governing principle that led to liturgical renewal and revision of the Order of the Mass. In the liturgy, the assembly does not become "strangers or silent spectators," but participants "in the sacred action, conscious of what they are doing, actively and devoutly."[189] With

---

[185] Jungmann, SJ, *The Mass,* 13.
[186] Hay, OFM, *Eucharist: A Thanksgiving Celebration,* 41.
[187] Ibid., 42.
[188] Vatican Council II, *Sacrosanctum Concilium*, no. 14.
[189] Ibid, no. 48

the procession for the presentation of the gifts, the faithful are invited to take part and be part of the act of worship. Consequently, the bringing of the gifts by the faithful for the support of the Church and for the alleviation of the needs of the poor like the hungry is, in fact, active and conscious participation in the sacrificial offering of Christ. *Redemptionis Sacramentum* adds that when bringing the gifts to the altar, the gifts "must always be a visible expression of that true gift that God expects from us: a contrite heart, the love of God and neighbor by which we are conformed to the sacrifice of Christ."[190] Love of God and love of neighbor is the principle that occupies the faithful in presenting the gifts.

The GIRM no. 22 notes that "the faithful express their participation by making an offering." Thus, this active participation in the Mass as shown through the presentation of the gifts is a form of communion in the Body of Christ. The Body of Christ to be cared for are the poor, the hungry and the oppressed. As members of the Body of Christ, they are welcomed in the table fellowship prepared by Christ. It is in this radical table fellowship that constitutes the Body of Christ. In the same vein, the presentation of the gifts is more than just a ritual; it is meant for action. It is an action that leads the faithful to be in solidarity with the poor and hungry for Eucharist, according to Pope John Paull II, is a "project of solidarity for all humanity."[191] The rite of the presentation of the gifts, which offerings are intended to support the Church and the poor, teaches one to live in solidarity with the poor as Jesus, who is received in the Communion, takes upon himself the human poverty in order to encounter him with the poor and hungry.

Such an act of presenting the gifts, explained in the Introduction of the Order of Mass no. 105, is the "powerful expression of the participation of all present in the Eucharist and in the social mission of the Church."[192] Although active participation is manifested in the presentation of the gifts through bringing forth the gifts, it only becomes authentic and genuine when the communal act is expressed through commitment and love for the poor and hungry. In other words, the ritual gesture of the presentation of the gifts is not limited to the Rite of the Preparation of the Gifts per se. Its fullness and genuineness must be realized even outside the Mass where the social life of the Church is situated. This participation in the presentation of the gifts breaks individualism and indifference and creates love and affection towards the needy. It invites the faithful to become gifts and blessings to others which becomes evident in the procession for the presentation of the gifts.[193] Membership in the Body of Christ, therefore, implies active participation in the life and mission of the Church.

---

[190] Congregation for Divine Worship and the Discipline of the Sacrament, Instruction On Certain Matters to be Observed or to be Avoided Regarding the Most Holy Eucharist *Redemptionis Sacramentum* (March 24, 2004), no. 70, (MA: Pauline Books and Media, 2004).

[191] John Paull II, Encyclical on Stay With Us Lord *Mane Nobiscum Domine* (7 October 2004) no. 27, London: Catholic Truth Society, 2004).

[192] Foley, *A Commentary on the General Instruction of the Roman Missal*, 166.

[193] Cecilia Payawal, PDDM, "Blessed are you, Lord of all creation!": A comparative study of the Rite of Preparation of the Gifts in the Roman and Byzantine Eucharistic Celebration, (Manila: San Beda College: Graduate School of Liturgy), 78.

3.3. Symbolism of Bread and Wine

The elements of bread and wine which are offered to the altar during the presentation of the gifts are rich in symbolism. Of course, these two elements affirm the goodness of God for gifting the world with gifts and all have an equal right to enjoy the goods of creation. But the bread and wine awaken the people's consciousness about the need for food during global hunger. In fact, when the *berakah* prayer is uttered by the priest, he says that the bread is the "fruit of the earth and work of human hands" and the wine is the "fruit of the vine and work of human hands." The bread and wine tell something about the toil and sweat, the pain and joy, and the fruits of labor, the human sinfulness, broken world, and the hunger experience.[194] Benedict XVI continues this line of thought, "In the bread and wine that we bring to the altar, all creation is taken up by Christ the Redeemer to be transformed and presented to the Father. In this way, we also bring to the altar all the pain and suffering of the world, in the certainty that everything has value in God's eyes."[195]

Yet, the bread and wine presented to the altar are transformed to become "the bread of life" and "the spiritual drink." Christ, the Bread of Life, who gives himself as the food and drink to be eaten and consumed makes it possible for the abundance to triumph over starvation and hunger.[196] In the Eucharist, Jesus becomes a source of nourishment for a hungry person who seeks for nourishment. Phillipe Rouillard notes that in receiving the bread and wine in the Eucharist: "I nourish myself with the life of the wheat and grapes sacrificed for me but also with the body of Christ given for me and with his blood shed for me."[197] Through his *kenosis* on the cross, Christ makes the abundance of life offered to all.[198] This self-emptying of Christ is made present in the celebration of the Eucharist for "each celebration of the Eucharist makes sacramentally present the gift that the crucified Lord made of his life, for us and for the whole world."[199] Hence, bread and wine are "both symbolic of the triumph of life."[200] Lauren Murphy further tells that "the use of bread and wine, therefore, announce the life that Christ offers to all people: the rich and poor, the filled and hungry, the employed and unemployed alike."[201] Thus, the Church, the Sacrament of Christ, must be eucharist to all by becoming food for the hungry and drink for the thirsty.

---

[194] William Marrevee, *The Popular Guide to the Mass* (Washington: The Pastoral Press, 1992), 80.

[195] Benedict XVI, Apostolic Exhortation On the Eucharist as the Source and Summit of the Church's Life and Mission *Sacramentum Caritatis* (Pasay City: Paulines, 2007), no. 47 (Pasay City: Paulines, 2007).

[196] Lauren Murphy, "Overcoming the Division: The Relationship between Eucharist and Social Justice," Theology Graduate Theses, Providence College, 2014, 44, http://digitalcommons.providence.edu/theology_graduate_theses/6 (accessed October 2, 2018).

[197] Phillipe Rouillard, "From Human Mean to Christian Eucharist," in *Living Bread, Saving Cup,* ed. R. Kevin Seasoltz (Collegeville, MN: The Liturgical Press, 1987), 128.

[198] Murphy, *Overcoming the Division: The Relationship between Eucharist and Social Justice,*

[199] *Sacramentum Caritatis,* no. 88.

[200] Ibid., no. 88.

[201] Ibid., no. 88.

3.4. Neglect of the social dimension of the rite in the Philippine Church

At the outset, the rite of presentation of the gifts is imbued with social dimension as the people take part in the liturgy by bringing bread and wine as well as to make liturgical collections for the needy. Other material gifts are offered too by the faithful. The social dimension of the rite dominated the public worship of the faithful.

Yet in the Philippines, the social dimension of the presentation of the gifts is seemingly neglected today. While there are some places in the country like Ifugao where baskets of fruits and vegetables are brought forward in a festive procession, there are some places where only the bread and wine are brought to the altar and few people bring gifts for the poor. In other parishes, they give their donations to the parish which add to the income but bypass the ritual action of giving. Taking up a collection within the Mass is always fitting and significant. Or a big chunk of the first collection is used for the upkeeping of the Church while a small amount is shared to the needy. Due to lack of liturgical catechesis, the faithful neglect to appreciate the value and meaning of the gifts presented to the altar. Some priests have not taken to heart the desired purpose of the gifts as material gifts offered to the poor are not shared. Although the GIRM says that the money or gifts are intended for the church and for the poor, the gifts for the poor are oftentimes disregarded.

What is needed is to recover the social dimension of the rite of the presentation of the gifts in the Philippine liturgy. The social meaning of the rite plays an important role in addressing hunger and other social problems that are existing in the society. The faithful's expression of their participation at Mass is by offering gifts for the needy. What gives significance to the social meaning of the rite is the concern for the needy and less privileged.

Conclusion

In this chapter, we have traced the historical development of the rite of the presentation of the gifts. This is dealt with presenting the biblical foundation of offering in the Old Testament in which the first fruits are offered in the temple as an act of worship and thanksgiving. Then, discipleship and table sharing in the Gospels are central too in the public ministry of Jesus. In Paul's understanding on the breaking of the bread, it is characterized by communion and concern to the poor.

Then, we have studied the historical development of the rite of the presentation of the gifts. The Church Fathers from Justin the Martyr to Cyprian had greatly contributed to the development of the rite by their rich theological understanding on the Eucharist. Also, the offertory is developed in the Western Liturgy until its decline in the Middle Ages. However, this rite has been reformed in the New Order of the Mass.

CHAPTER 3

Recovering the Significance of the Rite of Presentation of the Gifts in Addressing Hunger in the Philippines

Human hunger is a problem that the Philippines is facing now despite the strong presence of Christianity. Seemingly, the disparity between public worship and social responsibility is wide due to the increasing rate of poverty and hunger in the country. The Eucharist is the source and summit of Christian life; thus, it must significantly transform the Eucharistic value of fraternal sharing, communion, and solidarity with the poor and hungry. In the rite of the presentation of the gifts, these values are lived and experienced to end hunger and poverty.

This chapter explores the significance of Ubi Caritas and the collection of the gifts during Holy Thursday. The social themes of the rite with special emphasis on solidarity and social justice are discussed. It also suggests some pastoral actions which are necessary to end hunger. In order not to shun away from its spirituality, the chapter ends with a discussion on the spirituality of the rite.

1. Significance of *Ubi caritas, Deus ibi est*

In the liturgy for Holy Thursday, a Latin chant *Ubi Caritas* composed in the ninth century is sung during the Washing of the Feet at the Mass of the Last Supper. However, the Roman Missal 1970, 3rd Typical Edition 2000, transferred the antiphon from the *mandatum* to the offertory procession of Maundy Thursday.[202]

The rite of washing feet during the Mass of the Lord's Supper expresses a symbolic action of service and love for one another. It is not just an act of service but an act which "reveals the true nature of Christian love and discipleship."[203] In order to express one's loving service to others, the liturgy provides a special procession with the gifts for the poor. These gifts are not ordinary because they are the "fruits of sweat and toil."[204] The gifts are set aside for the poor during the presentation of the gifts and *Ubi Caritas* is a song that accompanies the procession. *Ubi Caritas* is rich in its text that motivates the people to bring gifts for the poor out of love and charity for love gives sense to the rite of the presentation of the gifts.

---

[202] For a complete text of Ubi Caritas, see Appendix,

[203] Thursday of the Lord's Supper: At the Evening Mass, *Roman Missal,* Ammended Latin Third Typical Edition (Manila: Catholic Bishops' Conference of the Philippines, 2011), 266

[204] Anscar J. Chupungco, *Towards A Filipino Liturgy* (Manila: Benedictine Abbey, 1976), 118.

However, this love comes from God and is shared to others especially the poor and the hungry through the gifts. Christ's love brings together the people into one in the Eucharist. It is by the love of Christ that true happiness is ultimately experienced. So, it is not greed, selfishness, power and injustice unto others that gladness and pleasure are found; it is love in God and charity for the poor and hungry. Therefore, when the people gather in Christ through the Eucharist, let the love of God dwell in each race and every person so that social injustices and indifference towards the poor and hungry cease. Social divisions, envy, strife, and hatred must end; fraternal sharing, social justice, and communion must thrive in each person. Fraternal sharing and communion in the Eucharist are concretized by the collection of the gifts for the poor on Holy Thursday celebration.

2. An Act of Service and Love: Collection of the gifts for the poor on Maundy Thursday

The Circular Letter of the Congregation for Divine Worship says that "gifts for the poor, especially those collected during Lent as the fruit of penance, may be presented in the offertory procession..."[205] Take note however that gifts are the "fruit of penance." After forty days of sacrifices, these sacrifices are offered to God in love and service to the poor. Though the faithful give the collection of gifts for the poor every day in the Mass, this profoundly Christian calling is greatly underscored on Holy Thursday. Christian love is further expressed through bringing gifts for the poor in the Mass. Hence, this offering is different from other ordinary Sunday collections because "it has a personal touch and the amount given is a part of our heart and our person, the result of our Lenten conversion."[206] In other words, it is an act of sacrifice.

Furthermore, the collection of gifts for the poor during Holy Thursday as suggested by the Roman Missal is interpreted as a real act of service that brings into practice the *Mandatum* of the Gospel to love one another as Christ has loved us.[207] Such real act of service is inspired by the text of one of the antiphons that can be chanted during the rite of washing the feet:

Mandatum novum do vobis ut diligatis invicem sicut dilexi vos ut et vos diligatis invicem. In hoc cognoscent omnes quia mei discipuli estis si dilectionem habueritis ad invicem.[208]

---

[205] Sacred Congregation for Divine Worship, *Circular Letter Concerning for the Preparation and Celebration of the Easter Feasts,* (January 16, 1988), no. 52.

[206] Bernhard Raas, SVD, *Liturgical Year: Volume 2* (Manila: Logos Publication, 1998), 117.

[207] Cf. John 13:4-17

[208] A new commandment I give to you, that you love one another: just as I have loved you, you also are to love one another. By this all people will know that you are my disciples, if you have love for one another. (John 13:34-35).

This collection as an act of penance, love, and service, is a special collection for the poor. The GIRM no. 73 notes that the recipients of the objects collected during the presentation of gifts in the Mass are the poor and the Church. Similarly, the rubrics for the Mass of the Lord's Supper on Holy Thursday states that the gifts presented are for the poor. Here, only the poor and not the Church are mentioned to be the recipients of the gifts collected. Love, sacrifice and service are important Eucharistic values which govern the liturgical act of presenting the gifts for the poor.

On the one hand, the collection of the gifts for the poor at Mass is a concrete act that may help to alleviate the hunger situation in the Philippines. This collection may be used for programs and activities of the Catholic community to respond to the problem of hunger in the country. It is not only used for the upkeeping of the Church; it must be utilized for pastoral actions which mitigate hunger in various parishes and dioceses. On the other hand, the values of love, sacrifice, and service of the presentation of the gifts are the values that must be inculcated in the hearts of the people as they bring their gifts to the altar during Mass. These values vouchsafe that social injustice and inequality of the goods of the earth can never thrive. The Filipinos need to love, sacrifice, and serve their fellow Filipinos so that hunger in the country is eased out.

There is no scarcity of food in the country because the Philippines is rich in resources. Men and women have enough food to eat in the country; yet few people take the food for themselves. Greed, selfishness, and gluttony are the sins that bring the people to hunger. The rich are festively enjoying the food while others are starved to death. The rite of the presentation of the gifts leads the people to conversion of heart and social transformation. Love and service are values which build a human society that is free from hunger and poverty. Solidarity and social justice too are important themes that can be learned from the presentation of the gifts.

3. Social Themes of the Rite of the Presentation of the Gifts

The rite of the presentation of the gifts is rich in its social themes which are important to reduce hunger in the country. These social themes like solidarity and social justice are two themes which can be deduced from the rite itself.

3.1. Sense of Solidarity

The *Constitution of the Sacred Liturgy* affirms that all liturgical celebrations are "an action of Christ the priest and of His Body which is the Church..."[209] This means that the Eucharist is not merely a private devotion but an act of the entire people of God. The relationship between liturgy and social action can only be established if the sense of solidarity is evolved. This principle of solidarity has found its ways into the Social

[209] Vatican Council II, *Sacrosanctum Concilium*, no. 7.

Encyclicals like *Rerum Novarum*, *Quadragesimo Anno*, *Populorum Progressio*, *Laborem Excercens*, *Sollicitudo Rei Socialis*, among others. *Sollicitudo Rei Socialis* notes that solidarity is not a feeling of vague compassion or shallow distress at the misfortunes of so many people, both near and far. On the contrary it is a firm and persevering determination to commit oneself to the common good. This is to say to the good of all and of everyone, because we are all really responsible for all."[210] Solidarity breaks the divisions in the world, between the rich and the poor. It encourages the rich to be responsible for the poor. It calls on the powerful to take care of those who are vulnerable and socially excluded in the community. Benedict XVI has this to say:

> It means a sense of individual awareness, of reciprocal responsibility; it means we are conscious that when we give we receive, and that we can always give only what has been given to us and that what we have been given never belongs to us for ourselves alone.[211]

This solidarity has become a significant principle in Catholic Social Thought. It has become a principle that is used in every realm of Christian life including the liturgy. The sense of solidarity is very much alive in the rite of the presentation of the gifts. The ritual of the presentation of the gifts has developed a culture of solidarity among the members of the Body of Christ. Paul's concern on the social division between the rich and poor which is contrary to the nature of eucharistic meal, the early Christians' concern of the poor through offering of gifts in the eucharist for their survival and the revival of the gifts for the poor which is lost in the Middle Ages- these are instances in the history of Christian worship that substantiate the development of solidarity in the public worship. From the historical development of the offertory, one can see that the commitment to give oneself for the good of others, especially the poor is present in the fundamental nature of the rite itself. Such an ethical principle of solidarity is an important dimension that is inherited in the rite per se. For Pope Francis, the Eucharist is the "school of charity and solidarity."[212] It is in the Eucharist that human solidarity is especially manifested because the goods of the earth and the labor of human work are shared to the needy.

In the country today, the incidence of hunger has increased. More and more people are suffering from hunger everyday as if caring is nonexistent. In the streets of Metro Manila alone, many children are loitering and begging for money to survive from starvation. People are interested in showbiz happenings but seldom when it matters to

---

[210] *Sollicitudo Rei Socialis,* no. 38.

[211]Benedict XVI, Lecture at the Bishops' Conference of the Region of Campania in Benevento (Italy) on the "Eucharist, Communion and Solidarity," https://w2.vatican.va/contevatican/en.html (accessed 7 December 2018).

[212] Francis, "Homily Mass, Procession to Saint Mary Major and Eucharistic Blessing on the Solemnity of the Most Holy Body and Blood of Christ," https://m.vatican.va/content/francescomobile/en/homilies/2015/documents/papa-francesco_20150604_omeilia--corpus-domini.htmly. (accessed 4 December2018).

hunger in the society. If only the people live up to the value of solidarity, then less people would live in hunger situations. This sense of solidarity is a value that one can deduce from the presentation of the gifts in the Mass. As such, one contends that the Filipinos must bring this moral virtue in their Eucharistic life so that it can help to mitigate hunger in the country.

3.2. Social Justice

The theme of social justice has received some attention in the Second Vatican Council. For instance, in the *Gaudium et Spes* notes that the "equal dignity of human beings, in virtue of their divine calling and destiny, demands that excessive economic and social disparity between individuals and peoples be eradicated."[213] In other words, the excessive social divisions in the society are contrary to equality. It notes further that "the best way to fulfil one's obligations of justice and love is to contribute to the common good according to one's means and the needs of others."[214] Yet it is important to understand that the foundation and motivation of all the social principles like human dignity, equality, and common good is the recognition that God is a God of justice. The liberating justice of God is significantly working in human history in the events of daily life, work of Christian people, and Christian worship. The justice of God is revealed in the liturgy and liturgy becomes the celebration of the justice of God.[215] As a celebration of God's justice, the liturgy "serves as a basis for social criticisms by giving us a criterion by which to evaluate the events and structures of the world."[216] In short, liturgy and justice must go together.

Given this understanding, one can ask: how does social justice manifest and appreciate in the celebration of the Mass? How is social justice to be done concretely? The answer to this problem lies on the purpose of the liturgical collection and presentation of the gifts. One important theme to be deduced from the presentation of the gifts is the theme on social justice. During the first three centuries, the close link between liturgy and social justice is expressed through the offering of material gifts.[217] The Eucharist is understood as "sacrifice of thanksgiving by which the participants expressed their membership in the new People of God."[218] The sacrificial gifts aside from the bread and wine offered by the faithful for God are expressions of their praise and thanksgiving to God and of concern for the needy.[219] Their offering of gifts becomes the fulfilment of their social obligations in the community. Of course, the material gifts

---

[213] *Gaudium et Spes,* no. 29.

[214] *Gaudium et Spes,* no. 30.

[215] Mark Seale, "Serving the Lord with Justice," in Mark Seale (ed.) *Liturgy and Social Justice,* (Collegeville, MN: Liturgical Press, 1980), 29.

[216] Ibid.

[217] Kilmartin, "The Sacrifice of Thanksgiving and Social Justice," 69.

[218] Kilmartin, "The Sacrifice of Thanksgiving and Social Justice," 69.

[219] Ibid., 58.

offered by the faithful are not in exchange to God's blessings; rather they are distributed to the poor as a fulfillment of their social obligations.

However, this was changed during the Middle Ages when the celebration of the Mass became the liturgy of the priest. On the one hand, the "gifts are added to a unified sacrificial act performed by the priest on behalf of the people."[220] On the other hand, the "gifts are a symbolic expression of the act of thanksgiving in which all co-offer to the Eucharist."[221] But what is common between these two views is the recognition that the faithful's offerings in the Mass signify the expression of unification of their life and work into the prayer of thanksgiving in the Eucharist.[222] Thus, the offering of gifts "expresses the consecration of one's whole life and work, including the fulfilment of social obligation before God."[223] In other words, Edward Kilmartin contends that presentation of the gifts is an invitation to consecrate one's life and work to God. It further illustrates that the rite underscores the relationship between social actions and the Eucharist.

The strong emphasis on the link between social action and Eucharist places the poor as the primary and normal recipients of the gifts offered in the presentation of the gifts. The gifts offered are not simply intended for the needs of the Church; the primary recipients of the Mass collection are the poor. Johannes Emminghaus argues that "there is a good foundation for the custom in some places of putting collection baskets next to the altar: this practice expresses the connection between the Eucharist and care for the poor."[224] The Letter to the Hebrews is a reminder for the faithful: "Through him let us continually offer God a sacrifice of praise, that is, the fruit of lips which acknowledge his name. Do not neglect good works and generosity: God is pleased with sacrifices of that kind."[225]

The problem of hunger is also attributed to the lack of social justice. The rite of the presentation of the gifts must lead to an effective action for justice to alleviate hunger in the country. The Church in the Philippines has been filled with churchgoers every Sunday and yet the social obligation to respond to the suffering of the hungry people is sometimes neglected. Social justice demands that the people should make financial sacrifices. The gifts offered and the collection at Mass is an opportunity for the faithful to exercise their social responsibility towards the hungry. What the faithful present as gifts to God are expressions of their sacrifices to make for social justice.

---

[220] Ibid., 70.
[221] Ibid., 70.
[222] Ibid., 70.
[223] Ibid., 70.
[224] Johannes H. Emminghaus, *The Eucharist: Essence, Form, Celebration*, 166.
[225] Hebrews 13:15-16

4. Pastoral Actions

Joseph Grassi contends that "painful hunger is a daily occurrence that must be countered by ongoing effective programs that enter into the lives of every Christian."[226] This means that Christians have an important role to play to alleviate hunger. Pastoral actions and initiatives are necessary to address human misery like hunger. These concrete actions intend to reduce the gravity of hunger problem through conscientization, an action-oriented liturgy which challenges the people to commitment to social problems and establish a ministry that is abreast to the current situation.

4.1. Liturgical Catechesis on the Presentation of the Gifts

Catechesis is "the process of transmitting the Gospel, as the Christian community has received it, understands it, celebrates it, lives it and communicates it in many ways."[227] In the Apostolic Exhortation *Catechesi Tradendae*, Pope John Paul II makes an important insight on the relationship between catechesis and liturgy. He said that "catechesis is intrinsically linked with the whole of liturgical and sacramental activity."[228] Anscar Chupungco contends that the "whole of liturgical and sacramental activity" includes the ritual celebration.[229] The catechesis on the prayers, texts and symbols of liturgy are of great value so that the faithful are directed towards an "active, conscious, and genuine participation" in the liturgy.

The liturgical catechesis on the rite of the presentation of the gifts is significant in the parish. This liturgical catechesis prepares the faithful to participate in the celebration of the Eucharist with special attention to the presentation of the gifts. The faithful must understand and recognize the symbols, the rituals, and prayers in the celebration. Also, it is important that the faithful who come to celebrate in the Eucharist are properly disposed. The liturgical catechesis does not only give catechetical instructions about the presentation of the gifts but it leads the worshipping community to an experience of conversion, fidelity to God's will, and the longing to be in conformity with Christ and his Church. More importantly, the liturgical catechesis prepares the faithful to a deeper appreciation of the social dimension of the rite so that eventually they are challenged to fulfil their social obligation of helping the poor. With a full understanding of the teachings that the rite per se contains, the faithful are drawn to an active participation in the Mass.

---

[226] Grassi, *Broken Bread and Broken Bodies: The Lord's Supper and World Hunger*, 93.

[227] Congregation for the Clergy, *General Directory for Catechesis*, (Washington DC: USCCB Publishing, 1998), 105.

[228] John Paul II, Apostolic Exhortation Catechesis in Our Time *Catechesi Tradendae*, no. 23 (Boston, MA: Pauline Books and Media, 1993).

[229] Anscar Chupungco, *Liturgy for the Filipino Church*, ed. Josefina Manabat, (Manila: San Beda Graduate School of Liturgy, 2014), 364.

How does liturgical catechesis on the rite of the presentation of the gifts be promoted in the parish? First, organize faith formation on the rite itself. *Christifideles Laici* reminds the faithful: "Formation is not the privilege of a few, but a right and duty of all."[230] Educating the faithful on the rite may encourage them to actively participate in the celebration. However, it is not only the rite itself but also to raise the people's awareness on hunger and the problems related to it. Part of the formation is the need for on-going conscientization. The people need a serious analysis of the situation. The faith formation, therefore, focuses on the relationship between the rite of the presentation of the gifts and hunger. Aside from the basic formation, the parish may also distribute pamphlets, brochures and so forth to educate the people. Education of the people is significant to open their eyes on the harrowing problem of hunger and how liturgy becomes relevant to this social concern.

4.2. Action-oriented liturgy

One challenging problem of the liturgy today is the obsession with rubrics. Seemingly, a correct observance of rubrics is needed for a dignified celebration of the liturgy. This is called rubricism in which "the celebrant's attention was fully engaged by the servile performance of every rubrical detail."[231] The *Redemptionis Sacramentum* affirms the rigidity in the rubrics when it "speaks of infractions and delicts in the liturgy that merit corresponding censure."[232] Of course, rubrics are important for it leads to the profound experience of Christ's mystery. The Constitution of the Liturgy, article 11, says that "when the liturgy is celebrated something more is required than the mere observance of the laws governing valid and lawful celebration."

What is that something more? That something 'more' is the link of worship with social justice. Instead of stressing on the rubrics in the celebration, one can significantly focus on the need for an action-oriented liturgy. Tissa Balasuriya has this to say:

> If Christian communities are to participate in the on-going revolutionary struggles for a better world, the liturgy must be related to them. The weekly gatherings for worship are the principal occasions when Christians meet. At present they are geared to action, but this is in connection with church-centered projects: church feasts, and the work of parish associations. The need is to link more seriously from poverty, oppression, affluence, lack of freedom, and so forth.[233]

---

[230] John Paul II, Post-Synodal Apostolic Exhortation on The Lay Members of Christ's Faithful People , *Christifideles Laici*, no. 63 (Boston, MA: Pauline Books and Media), 1989).

[231] Chupungco, *Liturgy for the Filipino Church,* 169.

[232] Ibid., 170.

[233] Tissa Balasuriya, *The Eucharist and Human Liberation,* (New York: Orbis Books, 1979), 140.

Liturgical display is not the primary concern of the church; rather it is an action-oriented liturgy that motivates the faithful to undertake relevant actions in their daily life for the eradication of human misery. To motivate the faithful to respond to the serious problem of hunger, the Prayer over the Offering must reflect the vision for solidarity and social justice towards the hungry. It is not only a prayer invoking God to sanctify the gifts offered and make them holy so that they are worthy of offerings. Kevin Irwin observes:

> that many of the prayers over the gifts are proleptic, which is to say that they anticipate the transformation of the gifts into Christ's body and blood...It would seem appropriate that some of these prayers speak directly to the sacramentality of creation and express how these humble gifts of bread and wine reflect service, homage, and honor to God the creator.[234]

Rather, it is a prayer that inspires those who are attending the Mass to transform themselves as gifts to the poor and the hungry. Also, the Offertory Chant is not only meant to accompany the ritual action. Its text must speak about the social situations of the poor and hungry who are deprived of the abundance of food and drink. Composers and musicians can create songs which instigate among the faithful the social justice and solidarity in the Body of Christ.

4.3. Soup Kitchen Ministry

Ministry comes from the Latin word "ministerium" which means to render service to others. As a member of the Body of Christ, one must have the loving interest to extend help and care for others for Jesus came not to be served but to serve. The Church is filled with various liturgical ministries like greeters and collectors, lectors and commentators, Eucharistic ministers, and altar servers, among others. But these ministries only focus on liturgical functions. Although these ministries are important in the liturgical life of the parish, it is also good to create a ministry that is responsive to social concerns in the community. This ministry in the community is characterized by *diakonia* where the community must 'go to the peripheries' to serve the people and not only to cater to the people's spiritual needs but also their material needs. However, it is good to note that this ministry is not meant to solve the whole problem of hunger; it is a way of presenting the love of God to others. It is to show concrete to the needy.

Hence, the Soup Kitchen Ministry is established. The primary function of this ministry is to uplift the hungry from socio-economic poverty, to bring back the dignity that is lost due to greed, to give hope to the hungry through kindness and hospitality and

---

[234] Kevin W. Irwin, "The Critical Task of Liturgical Theology: Prospects and Proposals" in *Eucharist: Toward the Third Millennium,* ed. Martin F. Connell, (Liturgy Training Publications, 1997), 18.

to motivate the hungry toward self-sufficiency. Thus, the Soup Kitchen Ministry develops an ongoing concern for the hungry through actions as an expression of one's solidarity and communion to the hungry. It intends to plan and organize effective and concerted efforts to alleviate hunger in the community. It organizes activities to generate funds, acquire food and donations for plentiful and nourishing food like the manna in the dessert. One possibility to acquire food is to encourage the faithful to bring gifts and offer them during the presentation of the gifts in the Mass. These gifts are used to feed the hungry in the community. In this way, the people have directly participated in all efforts to address hunger in the society. The spirit of the rite of the presentation of the gifts is evident when people come together to bring social transformation in the society through this ministry.

Another possibility is to allocate funds for the Soup Kitchen Ministry. A certain percent of the collection is allocated for the feeding program and other activities which mitigate hunger in the parish. The funds for the social services for the hungry must come directly from the collection during the offertory rite so that the faithful may have a sense of participation in the sacred works of charity as an expression of their concern and love for the needy. Although the collections are meant for the poor and other needs of the Church, it must be allocated so that the social services for the needy are rendered equally. In this way, the decent support of the clergy and construction projects are not merely the priority of the parish but also other works of charity toward the needy. Finally, Paul's statement in the *Second Letter to the Corinthians* is a motivation to carry out this ministry: "the love of Christ urges us on."[235]

5. Spirituality of Rite of the Presentation of the Gifts

Spirituality is a way of life that is directed by the Spirit. Surely, there are various spiritualities like the Vincentian spirituality, Ignatian spirituality, ecological spirituality, among others. These are different paths of encountering God and ways of following Christ. But what is more important is Paul's command to the disciples of Jesus: "walking according to the Spirit."[236] Paul's words mean that the life one has to embark is a life proper to what disciple of Jesus is and other ways of life which oppose such encounters with Jesus are to be shunned away. It is a life that lives in and according to the Spirit. However, spirituality is incomplete when it is not grounded with others because God is encountered in others. In other words, what is needed is a Christian spirituality that responds to the issues posed by modern society as God dwells in the contemporary human situation. With the above explanation, what then are the spiritualities offered by the rite of the presentation of the gifts? There are two spiritualities which one can deal with: encounter with God and encounter with the neighbours.

---

[235] 2 Corinthians 5:14

[236] Romans 8:4

5.1. Encounter with God

Anscar Chupungco argues that "liturgy is an encounter with God."[237] What kind of encounter? One needs to understand that the liturgy is God's initiative, and the people respond.[238] *Dei Verbum* affirms: "In His goodness and wisdom, God chose to reveal Himself and to make known to us the hidden purpose of His will..."[239] It is God who takes the initiative freely and lovingly to reveal himself. The human response to God's revelation is the obedience of faith. *Dei Verbum* continues: "The obedience of faith must be given to God who reveals, an obedience by which man entrusts his whole self freely to God, offering the full submission of intellect and will to God who reveals."[240] In the Eucharist, God reveals himself freely and lovingly. The Constitution on Liturgy mentions several instances where Christ is made present in the Eucharist: in the Eucharistic species, in the person of his minister, in the proclamation of God's word, and in the assembly gathered for worship.[241] God who reveals himself is encountered in the rite of the presentation of the gifts under the species of bread and wine. The people's faith in the liturgy is an expression of their response to God's initiative. The act of submission and surrender to God is the best approach to God's presence.

In the New Testament, one remembers that Jesus calls the poor and socially excluded in the community to dine with him. These people responded faithfully to God's invitation and eventually followed him. In the liturgy, God takes the initiative, and the people respond which "forms the dialogical nature of the liturgy."[242] It is an encounter between God and the people. This encounter with God is an encounter with the Trinity. The Father has sent his only begotten Son to redeem the world, and the Son has fulfilled his mission by reconciling the world to God, then the Father sent through his glorified Son the Holy Spirit.[243] Hence, the liturgy is Trinitarian and the encounter with God in the liturgy is also Trinitarian.

Nonetheless, the dialogical character of the liturgy is evident in the presentation of the gifts. God as *Dominie Deus universi* provides the abundance of graces to the people. The Catechism of the Catholic Church has explained the reasons of calling God 'Father:' "God is the first origin of everything and transcendent authority; and that he is at the same time goodness and loving concern for all his children."[244] Everything comes from God. In the Roman Liturgy particularly in the prayers over the gifts, the prayers are directed to the Father. This is to show an "act of the Church to honor and praise God

---

[237] Anscar Chupungco, *What, Then, Is Liturgy? Musings and Memoir,* (Quezon City: Claretian Publications, 2010), 108.

[238] Keith F. Pecklers, SJ, *Worship: New Century Theology,* (Quezon City: Claretian Publication, 2004), 23.

[239] Vatican Council II, *Dei Verbum,* no. 2.

[240] Vatican Council II, *Dei Verbum,* no. 5.

[241] Vatican Council II, *Sacrosanctum Concilium,* no. 7.

[242] Pecklers, SJ, *Worship: New Century Theology*, 23.

[243] Chupungco, *What, Then, Is Liturgy? Musings and Memoir,* 109.

[244] *Catechism of the Catholic Church*, 2nd ed. (Washington, DC: United States Catholic Conference, 2000), 239.

for his marvelous works."[245] And so, when the prayer over the bread and wine "Blessed are you, Lord God of all creation" is recited, the faithful recognize the goodness of the Creator who creates the human beings and all creatures on earth.

The people's response to God's graciousness is the offering of gifts. In presenting these gifts to God, the purity of heart and mind are important. St. Irenaeus of Lyons has this to say:

> For we are to present an offering to God, and in all things, we are to be grateful to the Creator, doing so with a pure mind, in faith, without hypocrisy, with firm hope, in fervent love, being the first fruits, without hypocrisy, with firm hope, in fervent love, being the first fruits of his own creation. The church alone offers this pure oblation to the Creator, offering it with a thanksgiving that comes from his creation.[246]

However, it is not only the bread and wine which are offered in the Mass but the very oneself is taken up to God which is transformed in the Eucharistic praying and communion.[247] The offering of oneself to God is a living sacrifice to God. Paul, in his address to the Romans, says: "I urge you, therefore, by the mercies of God to offer your bodies as a living sacrifice, holy and pleasing to God, your spiritual worship."[248] And so, the new sacrifice of the Christian people is not the animal sacrifices offered in the Temple but "it is the very body of the Christian offered to God in a holy life."[249] In short, one's body becomes a living sacrifice. Jeremy Driscoll contends that the faithful "do not offer up their lives by themselves. They can only do it through, and with, and in Christ's offering.[250] The faithful bring their lives to God and let them be transformed into the very Christ they receive in communion. Submission and surrender to God's will follow. When there is self-offering and an act of submission to God's will, then there is self-transformation in which they become servants of God and servants in the society. In this way, there is the encounter between God and the people. God initiates to show his goodness to people through his creation and the people respond to this God's graciousness by offering themselves to God and allow themselves to be transformed by Him.

---

[245] Chupungco, *What, Then, Is Liturgy? Musings and Memoir,* 114.

[246] Edward Foley (ed.), *Commentary on the Order of Mass of the Roman Missal,* (Quezon City: Claretian Publication, 2012), 222.

[247] Ibid., 222.

[248] Romans 12:1

[249] Jeremy Driscoll, OSB, *What Happens at Mass,* (India: Asian Trading Corporation, 2011), 60.

[250] Ibid., 60.

5.2. Encounter with others

The encounter with God in the presentation of the gifts is an encounter with the love of God. Yet, this encounter with God in the Mass leads to an encounter with the members of Christ's body. Paul Bernier argues that "communion with Jesus is a communion in the whole Christ, body and members."[251] Union with Christ at the Lord's table is also a union with those whom he shares himself. As Paul says, "Because there is one bread, we who are many are one body, for we all partake of the one bread."[252] The members of Christ's body become one in love with God. Precisely, the Eucharist is called an agape because the faithful are "one body." In the Eucharist, therefore, there is oneness among the members of Christ's body.

The Letter of John says that "God loved us first."[253] And this love that is experienced at the Lord's table is a reminder for the people that his blessing is meant to be shared. The love of God is inseparable from the love of others just as an encounter with God is an encounter with others and an encounter with others is an encounter with God. John's phrase must be quoted here: "If you do not love your neighbour whom you see, how can you love God whom you do not see."[254] Of course, no one has ever seen God. But it does not make God unknown. God makes himself known through others. Yet, the intimate encounter with God determines the basis for the people's encounter with others. People learn to look at others not based on their preferences but from God's preferences. They share their love to others from the love they experience from God. When the people feed the hungry, they do it with the eyes of Christ. Therefore, an intimate relationship with God is much more important for a genuine and authentic relationship with others. Benedict XVI has this to say:

> Love of God and love of neighbor are thus inseparable, they form a single commandment. But both live from the love of God who has loved us first. No longer is it a question, then, of a "commandment" imposed from without and calling for the impossible, but rather of a freely bestowed experience of love from within, a love which by its very nature must then be shared with others.[255]

His point is that the love of God and love of neighbor is not a commandment that needs to be undertaken. It is rather experiential, that is, an experience within which is

---

[251] Paul Bernier, *Living the Eucharist: Celebrating its Rhythms in Our Lives,* (Mystic CT: Twenty-Third Publications, 2005), 79.

[252] 1 Cor. 10:17

[253] John 4:10

[254] 1 Jn. 4:20

[255] Benedict XVI, Encyclical On Christian Love *Deus Caritas Est,* (25 December 2005), no. 20 (Pasay City: Paulines, 2008),

shared with others. Love of neighbors is not something to be imposed; it is the result of their love and faith in God. This love of neighbor is a responsibility that belongs to all members of Christ's body for "within the community of believers there can never be room for a poverty that denies anyone what is needed for a dignified life."[256] In the presentation of the gifts, the expression for the love of a neighbor is the bringing forward of money. Against this background, the collection of money's deeper meaning is to help those who are in need. People cannot come to God and say that they love him without showing the love to their neighbor.

Conclusion

We have seen in this chapter that solidarity and social justice are two important themes recovered from the rite of the presentation of the gifts. Solidarity demands to exhibit firm commitment to the common good of the people. Also, there is no dichotomy between social justice and worship. Justice and liturgy are inseparable.

Then, the pastoral actions are also discussed in this chapter. Liturgical catechesis, action-oriented liturgy and soup-kitchen ministry are the proposed initiatives to undertake to address human misery like hunger.

The chapter ends with a note on the spirituality of the rite of the presentation of the gifts. This spirituality is both an encounter with God and encounter with others.

---

[256] *Deus Caritas Est*, no. 20.

SUMMARY AND CONCLUSION

Hunger has been a harrowing problem in various parts of the world. In Asia alone, more and more people are suffering from this problem. The Philippines too has not been liberated from this social concern as it continues to face it. Causes are identified and efforts have been made to end hunger in the country. The Philippine government has institutionalized policies and reforms which aimed at ensuring food availability for the people. Various non-government institutions too have made their efforts to completely end hunger. In the country where most of the people are Catholics, the Philippine Church has continued to reflect on hunger and awakened the slumbered consciousness of the people through pastoral letters and concrete actions. It challenges the people to actively participate in all actions which are meant to end hunger. Magisterial teachings are considered for a better judgment on hunger. The Church is rich in her doctrines and worship which are of great importance to recognize, reflect, and commit to action on hunger. Within the Church, the rite of the presentation of the gifts in the Eucharist plays a significant character in alleviating hunger.

Then, historical, and theological development of the rite of the presentation of the gifts has been dealt. The Old Testament and New Testament biblical types are investigated to understand offering, Jesus' table-sharing and discipleship. In the public ministry of Jesus, feeding the hungry is one of his commands. Also, Paul's breaking of the bread has placed the Christian communities into a community where there is sharing, solidarity and communion. The Fathers of the Church, from Justin the Martyr to Cyprian, have been analyzed. In the breaking of the bread, the concern for the poor and less privileged is significant to the celebration. In other words, the social dimension of the presentation of the gifts is evident as people have actively participated in the presentation of the gift. However, the social dimension was lost during the Middle Ages but only recovered in the Vatican II Council. In the theology of the presentation of the gifts, God is the source of all things. These gifts must also be shared to others in communion to the mystical Body of Christ. The change of the bread and wine into Body and Blood of Christ challenges the people to be *Christs* to others, especially the hungry.

Finally, the rite of the presentation of the gifts is imbued with social values which when applied to help, will end hunger in the country. These values are solidarity and a sense of social justice. If solidarity and a sense of social justice are developed, the rite itself will become a liberating action affecting the lives of the people. As such, the social values of the rite need to be dealt with to bring out the social relevance of the rite to the problem of hunger. Pastoral actions too are necessary to highlight these social values. These pastoral actions are the liturgical catechesis, action-oriented liturgy, and establishment of soup kitchen ministry. The spiritual dimension of the rite is also included in the discussion.

Against this background, it is interesting to note that the rite of the presentation of the gifts contributes to the critique of the hunger situation in the country. That is the stand of this research study. It is no longer ritualistic but a ritual that entails actions highlighting the social and practical dimensions and its implication to the praxis of the people. The rite is not to be restricted within the performance of the rubrics or doctrinal formulations; it must be appreciated within the realm of hunger. The presentation of the gifts is not just a rite; it is an action. In other words, the rite must be relevant to the liberation of the slavery of the hungry people.

BIBLIOGRAPHY

1. Books

Balasuriya, Tissa. *The Eucharist and Human Liberation.* New York: Orbis Books, 1979.

Ball, Nicole. *World Hunger: A Guide to the Economic and Political Dimensions.* Santa Barbara, Cali: American Bibliographical Center, Clio Press, 1981.

Beckmann, David, Simon, Arthur. *Grace at the Table: Ending Hunger in God's World. New* York: Paulist Press,1999.

Bernier, Paul. *Living the Eucharist: Celebrating its Rhythms in Our Lives.* Mystic CT: Twenty-Third Publications, 2005.

Boselli, Goffredo. *The Spiritual Meaning of the Liturgy: School of Prayer, Source of Life.* trans. Barry Hudock. Collegeville, MN: Liturgical Press, 2014.

Brown, R., Fitzmyer, J., Murphy, R., Eds., *The New Jerome Biblical Commentary.* Bangalore: Bangalore Theological Publications in India, 2013.

Bugnini, Annibale. *The Reform of the Liturgy 1948-1975.* Collegeville: The Liturgical Press, 1990.

Burghardt, Dillon, McManus. eds. *Ancient Christian Writers: The Works of Fathers* in Translation. *St. Justin Martyr: The First and Second Apologies.* trans. Leslie William Barnard.

Byron, J. William. *The Causes of World Hunger.* in *The Causes of World Hunger.* ed. William J. Byron. Ramsey, NJ: Paulist, 1982.

Cabie, Robert. *The Eucharist,* ed. Aime Georges Martimort, trans. Matthew O'Connel, *The Church at Prayer 2.* Collegeville, MN: Liturgical Press, 1986.

Carter, Warren. *Matthew and the Margins: A Sociopolitical and Religious Reading.* Maryknoll, New York: Orbis Books, 2000.

Chauvet, Louis-Marie. *Symbol and Sacrament: A Sacramental Reinterpretation of Christian Existence.* Collegeville, MN: Liturgical Press, 1995.

Chupungco, J. Anscar. *Liturgy for the Filipino Church.* ed. Josefina Manabat. Manila: San Beda Graduate School of Liturgy, 2014.

_____________.*What, Then, Is Liturgy? Musings and Memoir.* Quezon City: Claretian Publications, 2010.

_______________. *Towards A Filipino Liturgy.* Manila: Benedictine Abbey, 1976.

Crockett, William R. *Eucharist: Symbol of Transformation.* New York: Pueblo Publishing Company, 1989.

Driscoll, Jeremy. *What Happens at Mass.* India: Asian Trading Corporation, 2011.

Dix, Gregory. *The Shape of the Liturgy.* London: New York, 1945.

Elliot, J. Peter. Ceremonies *of the Modern Rite: The Eucharist and the Liturgy of the Hours,* San Francisco: Ignatius Press, 1995.

Emminghaus, H. Johannes. *The Eucharist: Essence, Form, Celebration.* Collegeville, MN: Liturgical Press, 1997.

Foley, Edward. ed. *Commentary on the Order of Mass of the Roman Missa.* Quezon City: Claretian Publication, 2012.

Grassi, Joseph. *Broken Bread and Broken Bodies: The Lord's Supper and World Hunger.* New York: Orbis Books, 1985.

Hay, Leo. *Eucharist: A Thanksgiving Celebration.* Washington Daleware: Michael Glazier, 1989.

Hellwig, Monika K. *The Eucharist and the Hunger of the World.* New York: Paulist Press, 1976.

Hexter, J.H. *The Judaeo-Christian Tradition,* 2nd ed. London: Yale University Press, 1966.

Javier, Francisco. *The Making of a Local Church.* Quezon City: Claretian Publication, 2009.

Jungmann, A. Josef. *The Mass.* Collegeville, Minnesota: The Liturgical Press, 1976.

Jungmann, Joseph. *The Mass of the Roman Rite: Its Origins and Development.* trans. Francis A. Brunner. London: Burns and Oats, 1959.

Kilmartin, J. Edward. *The Eucharist in the West: History and Theology.* ed. Robert J. Daly. Collegeville, MN: The Liturgical Press, 1998.

Klauser, Theodor. *A Short History of the Western Liturgy.* Oxford: Oxford University Press, 1979.

Kwiatkowski, M. Lynn. *Struggling with Development: The Politics of Hunger and Gender in the Philippines.* Manila: Ateneo de Manila University Press, 1999.

Marrevee, William. *The Popular Guide to the Mass.* Washington: The Pastoral Press, 1992.

Mauro, Paolo. *Causes and Consequences of Corruption.* in *Ehem!: A Manuel For Deepening Involvement in Combating Corruption,* 2nd ed. Quezon City: Philippine Province of the Society of Jesus, Committee on the Evangelization of Culture, 2003.

McCormick, T. Patrick. *A Banqueter's Guide to the All-Night Soup Kitchen of the Kingdom of God.* Collegeville, MN: Liturgical Press.

McGuckian, Michael. *The Holy Sacrifice of the Mass.* Chicago: Liturgy Training Publications, 2005.

Miller, CM, Charles. *The Celebration of the Eucharist.* vol. II. New York: Alba House, 2001.

O'Brien and Shannon. *Catholic Social Thought; Documentary Heritage.* New York: Orbis Books, 2010.

Parsch, Pius. *The Liturgy of the Mass.* trans. Rev. Frederick C. Eckhoff. London: B Herder Book Co, 1942.

Pecklers, F. Keith. *Worship: New Century Theology.* Quezon City: Claretian Publication, 2004.

Pilario, Daniel Franklin. ed. *Faith in Action: A Catholic Social Teaching on the Ground.* Quezon City: St. Vincent School of Theology, 2017.

Raas, Bernhard. *Liturgical Year: Volume 2.* Manila: Logos Publication, 1998.

Russell, C. James. *The Germanization of Early Medieval Christiantianity: A Sociohistorical Approach to Religious Transformation.* New York: Oxford University, 1994.

Sen, Amartya. *Development as Freedom.* New York: Anchor Books, 1999.

Sen, Amartya. *Poverty and Famines: An Essay on Entitlement and Deprivation.* London, New York, Toronto: Oxford University Press, 1984.

Witczak, Michael. *History of the Latin Text and Rite.* in *Commentary on the Order of Mass of the Roman Missal,* ed. Edward Foley. Quezon City: Claretian Publication, 2012.

2. Articles

Danilo, and Briones. "Impacts of Natural Disasters on Agriculture, Food Security, and Natural Resources." *Economic Research Institute for ASEAN and East Asia Discussion Paper Series 15*, 2013.

3. Articles in a Book

Bugnini, Annibale. *The New 'Ordo Missae.' "L'Osservatore Romano,"* May 22, 1969, 8, in *Eucharist: A Thanksgiving Celebration.* Leo Hay. Wilmington, Delaware: Michael Glazier, 1989.

Foley, Edward. *The Structure of the Mass, Its Elements and Its Parts.* in *Commentary on the General Instruction of the Roman Missal*, ed. Edward Foley. Collegeville, MN: Liturgical Press, 2007.

Irwin, W. Kevin. *The Critical Task of Liturgical Theology: Prospects and Proposals* in *Eucharist: Toward the Third Millennium.* ed. Martin F. Connell. Chicago: Liturgy Training Publications, 1997.

Justin Martyr, "First Apology Chapter 65," in *The Catholic Tradition: Mass and the Sacraments* Vol. 1. ed. Charles J. Dollen, et al, (America: Mc Grath Publishing Company, 1979.

Kilmartin, J. Edward . *The Sacrifice of Thanksgiving and Social Justice.* in *Liturgy and Social Justice.* ed. Mark Seale. Collegeville, MN: Liturgical Press, 1980.

Ledogar, J. Robert. *The Eucharistic Prayer and the Gifts Over which It is Spoken.* in *Living Bread and Saving Cup: Readings on the Eucharist.* ed. R. Kevin Seasoltz. Collegeville, Minnesota: Liturgical Press, 1982.

McManus, Frederick. *The Roman Order of Mass from 1964 to 1969: The Preparation of the Gifts.* in *Shaping English Liturgy*, eds. Peter Finn, James M. Schellman. Washington: The Pastoral Press, 1900.

Rouillard, Phillipe. *From Human Mean to Christian Eucharist.* in *Living Bread, Saving Cup,* ed. R. Kevin Seasoltz. Collegeville, MN: The Liturgical Press, 1987.

Seale, Mark. *Serving the Lord with Justice.* in *Liturgy and Social Justice.* ed. Mark Seale Collegeville, MN: Liturgical Press, 1980.

Shannon, Thomas. *Commentary on Rerum Novarum (The Condition of Labor).* in *Modern Catholic Social Teaching: Commentaries and Interpretations,* ed. Kenneth R. Himes. Washington: Georgetown University Press, 2011.

4. Church Documents

Benedict XVI. Encyclical Letter On Christian *Love Deus Caritas Est,* (25 December 2005). Pasay City: Paulines, 2008.

Benedict XVI. Encyclical Letter *Charity in Truth* Caritas in Veritate*,* (29 June 2009). Pasay City: Paulines 2009.

Benedict XVI, Apostolic Exhortation On the Eucharist as the Source and Summit of the Church's Life and Mission *Sacramentum Caritatis* (22 February 2007). Pasay City: Paulines, 2007.

Catechism of the Catholic Church. 2nd ed. (Washington, DC: United States Catholic Conference, 2000.

Catholic Bishops of the Philippines. *A Joint Pastoral Letter of the Catholic Bishops of the Philippines on Social Justice,* Manila: Catholic Bishops Conference, 1949.

Catholic Bishops' Conference of the Philippines. *Pastoral Statement of the Philippine Hierarchy on Year of Social Action.* Manila: Catholic Bishops Conference, 1968.

Congregation for Divine Worship and the Discipline of the Sacrament. On Certain Matters to be Observed or to be Avoided Regarding the Most Holy Eucharist *Redemptionis Sacramentum* (23 April 2004). MA: Pauline Books and Media, 2004.

Congregation for the Clergy. *General Directory for Catechesis.* Washington DC: USCCB Publishing, 1998.

International Commission on English in the Liturgy. "General Instruction on the Roman Missal." In Instructions on the Revised Roman Rites: Initiation, Roman Missal, Eucharist Outside Mass, Anointing and Pastoral Care of the Sick, Funerals, Marriage, Holy Order, Ministries, Blessing of Oils, Lectionary. London, Glasgow: Collins Liturgical Publications, 1979.

John Paul II. Apostolic Exhortation on Catechesis in Our Time *Catechesi Tradendae* (16 October 1979). Boston, MA: Pauline Books and Media, 1993.

John Paul II. Post-Synodal Apostolic Exhortation The Lay Members of Christ's Faithful People *Christifideles Laici* (30 December 1988). Boston, MA: Pauline Books and Media, 1989.

John Paul II. Apostolic Letter on Stay With Us Lord *Mane Nobiscum Domine* (7 October 2004). London: Catholic Truth Society, 2004.

John Paul II. Encyclical On the Social Concerns *Sollicitudo Rei Socialis* (30 December 1987). Boston, MA: Pauline Books and Media, 1987.

John Paul II. Encyclical Letter On the Eucharist in its Relationship to the Church *Ecclessia De Eucharistia* (17 April 2003). London: Catholic Truth Society, 2003.

Leo XIII. Encyclical Letter On the Condition of the Working Classes *Rerum Novarum* (15 May 1891). Boston, MA: Daughter of St Paul, 2000.

Paul VI. Encyclical Letter On the Development of Peoples *Populorum Progressio* (26 March 1976). Boston, MA: Daughter of St. Paul, 2000.

Sacred Congregation for Divine Worship. *Circular Letter Concerning for the Preparation and Celebration of the Easter Feasts* (20 February 1988). Vatican: Liberia Editrice, 1988.

Vatican Council II. Dogmatic Constitution on the Sacred Liturgy *Sacrosanctum Concilium* (4 December 1963). In Vatican Council II: The Conciliar and Post Conciliar Documents. ed. Austin Flannery. Pasay City: Paulines, 2006.

Vatican Council II. Pastoral Constitution on the Church in the Modern World *Gaudium et Spes* (7 December 1965). In Vatican Council II: The Conciliar and Post Conciliar Documents. ed. Austin Flannery, Pasay City: Paulines, 2006.

Vatican Council II. Dogmatic Constitution on the Church *Lumen Gentium* (21 November 1964). In Vatican Council II: The Conciliar and Post Conciliar Documents. ed. Austin Flannery. Pasay City: Paulines, 2006.

Vatican Council II. Dogmatic Constitution on Divine Revelation *Dei Verbum* (18 November 1965). In Vatican Council II: The Conciliar and Post Conciliar Documents. ed. Austin Flannery. Pasay City: Paulines, 2006.

5. Internet Sources

Benedict XVI, Lecture at the Bishops' Conference of the Region of Campania in Benevento (Italy) on the "Eucharist, Communion and Solidarity," https://w2.vatican.va/contevatican/en.html (accessed 7 December 2018).

Brown, Sophie. "The Philippines Is the Most Storm-Exposed Country on Earth." http://world.time.com/2013/11/11/the-philippines-is-the-most-storm-exposed-country-on-earth (accessed 3.8.2018).

Catholic Relief Services (CRS). https://www.interaction.org/member/catholic-relief-services (accessed 10.8.2010).

Francis, *Address to the United Nations' Food and Agriculture Organization on Word Food Day,* 16 October 2017, http://m.vatican.va/content/francescomobile_visita-fao.html (accessed 5.13.2018).

Francis. "Homily Mass, Procession to Saint Mary Major and Eucharistic Blessing on the Solemnity of the Most Holy Body and Blood of Christ." https://m.vatican.va/content/francescomobile/en/homilies/2015/documents/papa-francesco_20150604_omeilia--corpus-domini.htmly. (accessed 4 December2018).

Food and Agriculture Organization. "Rome Declaration on World Food Security and World Food Summit Plan of Action." http://www.fao.org/docrep/003/w3613e/w3613e00.html (accessed 21.3.2018).

Food and Agriculture Organization. "Sustainable Development Goals." https://unstats.un.org/sdgs/report/2016/goal-02/ (accessed 3.8.2018).

Garcia, Cesar. "Fast Facts: What Has the Government Done to Alleviate Malnutrition?." https://www.rappler.com/newsbreak/iq/208157-what-philippine-government-has-done-address-malnutrition (accessed 28.10.2018).

Leonen, N. Julius. "Hunger Falls in First Quarter of 2018-SWS." https://www.google.com.ph/amp/s/newsinfo.inquirer.net/986324/breaking-news-sws-hunger-rodrigo-duterte-gloria-macapagal-arroyo/amp (accessed 12.6.2018).

Mateo, Janvic. "SWS: 1 in 3 Families Move Out of Poverty," *The Philippine Star,* January 21, 2018, https://www.philstar.com/headlines/2018/01/21/1779850/sws-1-3-families-move-out-poverty, (accessed 12.7.2018).

Murphy, Lauren. "Overcoming the Division: The Relationship between Eucharist and Social Justice." http://digitalcommons,providence.edu/theology_graduate_thes (accessed October 2, 2018).

National Economic and Development Authority. "Ambisyon Natin 2014, A Long Term Vision for the Filipinos." http://2040.neda.gov.ph/about-ambisyon-natin-2040/ (accessed 3.8.2018).

National Nutrition Council. "Philippine Plan of Action for Nutrition 2017-2022." http://www.nnc.gov.ph/phocadownloadpap/PPAN/18Sept_PPAN2017_2022Executive%20Summary.pdf (accessed 19.5.2018).

Rey, Aika. "In Numbers: Impact of Corruption on the Philippines." *Rappler*, 10 August 2016. https://www.google.com.ph/amp/samp.rappler.com/move-(accessed 7.6.2017).

United Nations. "Universal Declaration on the Eradication of Hunger and Malnutrition." https://www.ohchr.org/en/professionalinterest/pages/eradicationofhungerandmalnutrition.aspx (accessed 7.21.2018).

World Bank. "FAQs About the Pantawid Pamilyang Pilipino Programs (4Ps)." https://www.worldbank.org/en/country/philippines/brief/faqs-about-the-pantawid-pamilyang-pilipino-program (accessed accessed 10.9. 2018).

6. Other sources

Briones, Roehlano et al. *Food Security and Nutrition in the Philippines.* Brain Trust, INC., 2017.

Food and Agriculture Organization (FAO). International Fund for Agricultural Development (IFAD) and World Food Programme (WFP). *The State of Food Insecurity in the World 2013: The Multiple Dimensions of Food Insecurity.* Rome: FAO, 2013.

Food and Agriculture Organization (FAO). International Fund for Agricultural Development (IFAD) and World Food Programme (WFP). United Nations Children's Fund (UNICEF), World Health Organization (WHO). *The State of Food Security and Nutrition in the World 2017.* Rome: FAO, 2017.

Food and Agriculture Organization (FAO). *Food Security Information for Action: Food Security Concepts and Framework.* European Union: FAO, 2008.

United Nations. *Basic Facts About the United Nations.* New York: United Nations Publication, 2004.

7. Articles

Concilium Matisconense (548), can. 4, ed. C. De Clercq, *Concilia Galliae* (CCL 148A), 240-41.

St Jerome, *In Hieremim Prophetam II*, 108, ed. S. Reiter (CCL 74; Turnhout: Brepols, 1960), 116; *idem, In Hezechielem Prophetam* VI, 16, ed. F. Glorie (CCL 75; Yurnhout: Brepols, 1964), 238.

Liber officialis III, 19, 4, 17, 36, in J. M. Hanssens, *Amalarii episcope opera liturgia omnia,* Studi e Testi 139 (Vatican City, 1948) 2:312, 316, 332).

Gregory of Tours, *Liber miraculorum in Gloria confessorum,* 64, ed. B. Krusch (MGH, Script. Aev. Merov.) 1 (1885) 785-86.

8. Unpublished material

Okonkwo, Izunna. "Transformative Power of the Eucharist with Special Attention to the Harrowing Problem of Hunger: A Theological Exploration with South East Nigeria as a Point of Reference." PhD. diss., Katholieke Universiteit Leuven, 2011.

Payawal, Cecilia PDDM. "Blessed are you, Lord of all creation!": A comparative study of the Rite of Preparation of the Gifts in the Roman and Byzantine Eucharistic Celebration. Manila: San Beda College: Graduate School of Liturgy.

Appendix

Ubi Caritas

UBI caritas et amor, Deus ibi est.
Congregavit nos in unum Christi amor.
Exultemus, et in ipso iucundemur.
Timeamus, et amemus Deum vivum.
Et ex corde diligamus nos sincero.

WHERE charity and love are, God is there.
Christ's love has gathered us into one.
Let us rejoice and be pleased in Him.
Let us fear, and let us love the living God.
And may we love each other with a sincere heart.

UBI caritas et amor, Deus ibi est.
Simul ergo cum in unum congregamur:
Ne nos mente dividamur, caveamus.
Cessent iurgia maligna, cessent lites.
Et in medio nostri sit Christus Deus.

WHERE charity and love are, God is there.
As we are gathered into one body,
Beware, lest we be divided in mind.
Let evil impulses stop, let controversy cease,
And may Christ our God be in our midst.

UBI caritas et amor, Deus ibi est.
Simul quoque cum beatis videamus,
Glorianter vultum tuum, Christe Deus:
Gaudium quod est immensum, atque probum,
Saecula per infinita saeculorum. Amen.

WHERE charity and love are, God is there.
And may we with the saints also,
See Thy face in glory, O Christ our God:
The joy that is immense and good,
Unto the ages through infinite ages. Amen.

www.ingramcontent.com/pod-product-compliance
Lightning Source LLC
LaVergne TN
LVHW060825170826
845678LV00010B/1903

* 9 7 8 1 0 6 8 8 3 9 5 0 4 *